CW01082601

# MAN
# OVERBOARD!

# MAN OVERBOARD!

*The Story of Jonah*

## Sinclair B. Ferguson

THE BANNER OF TRUTH TRUST

THE BANNER OF TRUTH TRUST
3 Murrayfield Road, Edinburgh EH12 6EL, UK
P.O. Box 621, Carlisle, PA 17013, USA

\*

First published 1981
First Banner of Truth edition 2008

© Sinclair B. Ferguson 2008

ISBN-13: 978 0 85151 982 1

\*

Typeset in 11/15 Adobe Caslon Pro at
the Banner of Truth Trust, Edinburgh

Printed in the U.S.A. by
Versa Press, Inc.,
East Peoria, IL

TO THE MISSIONARIES CALLED FROM
ST GEORGE'S-TRON CHURCH,
GLASGOW

'The word of the LORD came . . . Go . . .'

JONAH 1:1–2, 3:1–2

# CONTENTS

# PREFACE
## TO THE 2008 EDITION

In this new format, this brief exposition of the book of Jonah has – like Jonah himself – been brought back from the hidden depths. Out of print for perhaps two decades, it now reappears, in slightly different form, thanks to the encouragement of the Publisher's Editorial Director, Jonathan Watson. I am grateful to him for his insistence and persistence.

The book of Jonah is part of Holy Scripture. As such it is 'breathed out by God and profitable for teaching, for reproof, for correction, and for training in righteousness, that the man of God may be competent, equipped for every good work' (*2 Tim.* 3:16–17). The God-breathed narrative of Jonah accomplishes all four of these goals. Here we are taught how Jonah learned in a profound way the truth that runs like a plot-line through the Bible from Genesis to Revelation, 'Salvation belongs to the LORD' (*Jon.* 2:10). It was a sore lesson to learn and involved a very physical 'reproof'. But it also brought 'correction' in the sense Paul means – healing, restoration, and transformation. Jonah was thus trained in the gymnasium of God's special providences to be an obedient servant. He was equipped by what he learned about himself to bring the Word of God to a community of people to whom at times he bore an all too uncomfortable resemblance.

Here then is the message of God's sovereign grace, and all that flows from it, in the form of a short but vivid drama from the annals of Old Testament history. My prayer is that it will be for some readers the very word they most need to hear.

SINCLAIR B. FERGUSON
First Presbyterian Church
Columbia, S.C., U. S.A.
February 2008

# INTRODUCTION

Most people are fascinated by the story of Jonah. It is a very dramatic tale with all kinds of unusual features. But Jonah also lends itself to the kind of studies which the chapters of this short book contain.

For one thing, Jonah is biographical. Indeed it is in all probability autobiographical, although written in the third person. As is often the case with biblical biographies, we find ourselves and our own hearts mirrored in the experience of others. We learn from what they do, and we also learn from what they failed to do. The teaching of Jonah searches our hearts and consciences in a special way because it is the story of a man who was on the run from God. It traces not only the path of his journey, but unravels the inner workings of his heart – his fears, motivations, and passing moods. Christians today still experience these 'Jonah-syndromes'.

There is, however, another special value in the book of Jonah. As we shall discover, it is not a book about a great fish! It is really a book about God, and how one man came, through painful experience, to discover the true character of the God whom he had already served in the earlier years of his life. He was to find the doctrine about God (with which he had long been familiar) come alive in his experience. It is this combination of doctrine and experience that makes Jonah such a fascinating, instructive, and practical book.

The best sub-title for Jonah might be *Evangelism and the Sovereignty of God*, because it is these two biblical emphases which come to the fore throughout its pages. Jonah was forced to learn in his flight from God that God is sovereign. He rules over all things. He also learned that the pulse-beat of God's heart has an evangelistic rhythm. He loves men and women and he will pursue them with his love in order to bring them to repentance and faith.

Jonah speaks to the church at this level too. The doctrines of evangelism and divine sovereignty are on many Christians' lips today. Those who emphasize one *rather than* or even *against the other*, often find themselves breaking fellowship with their fellow Christians.

Sometimes those who emphasize evangelism see God's sovereignty as a barrier to it, and those who emphasize God's sovereignty are suspicious and fearful of evangelism. We are very human and frail! But the marvel of the biblical teaching is that God's sovereignty and our evangelism are married in beautiful harmony – as Jonah himself discovered at the most personal level. Few sections of Scripture emphasize so clearly that God is sovereign in all evangelism, and he is evangelistic in the exercise of his sovereignty.

In the light of this we will discover that Jonah is not only a book about personal spiritual experience. It is also a word which speaks to the missionary involvement of Christians. It presents to us a *cri de coeur* to lay aside all our reluctance and disobedience, and to fulfil our Lord's commission to preach the gospel to every creature. But Jonah also forewarns us of the kind of experience we may go through as a result. It shows us a picture of a very weak and inadequate vessel whom God used for his glory. Jonah was a man who, at the end of his term of missionary service (in fact, even before he had come home!), was on the verge of throwing in the towel. He became a servant of God totally dejected by his service.

*Introduction*

Here then is a book which speaks to the hearts of missionaries of Christ – a mini orientation course for overseas evangelism. Here too is a book which searches and cleanses the heart of every servant of Christ who is engaged in holding out the word of life to our world (*Phil.* 2:15–16).

In order to increase the convenience of using this study, each chapter is preceded by the relevant section of Jonah. It will greatly increase the value of this book if the section of Scripture is first carefully read.

It is my prayer for readers of these pages that this exposition of the experience of Jonah will allow the book that bears his name to speak to them. Jonah is part of God's Word to us, and God undoubtedly continues to speak through it. 'He who has ears to hear, let him hear.'

SINCLAIR B. FERGUSON

Glasgow
February 1981

I

# ALL IN THE PAST

*Now the word of the LORD came to Jonah the son of
Amittai, saying, ² 'Arise, go to Nineveh, that great city,
and call out against it, for their evil has come up before me.'
³ But Jonah rose to flee to Tarshish from the presence of
the LORD. He went down to Joppa and found a ship going to Tarshish. So he paid the fare and went on board, to go
with them to Tarshish, away from the presence of the LORD*
(Jon. 1:1–3).

Jonah! His name means *dove* in Hebrew, but how different from
the first dove which flew from the ark to find dry land where
the kingdom of God might be re-established after the judgment
of the flood.

Jonah! On reflection how little the Bible seems to say about
the details of his personal life. His own book identifies him in the
briefest and simplest of fashions:

Now the word of the LORD came to Jonah the son of Amittai,
saying, ² 'Arise, go to Nineveh, that great city . . .'

But these words at least provide a clue to enable us to track
down this elusive prophet of God. They identify him with the
Jonah who receives honourable mention in the Books of the
Kings:

In the fifteenth year of Amaziah the son of Joash, king of Judah, Jeroboam the son of Joash, king of Israel, began to reign in Samaria, and he reigned forty-one years. [24] And he did what was evil in the sight of the LORD. He did not depart from all the sins of Jeroboam the son of Nebat, which he made Israel to sin. [25] He restored the border of Israel from Lebo-hamath as far as the Sea of the Arabah, *according to the word of the LORD, the God of Israel, which he spoke by his servant Jonah the son of Amittai, the prophet, who was from Gath-hepher.* [26] For the LORD saw that the affliction of Israel was very bitter, for there was none left, bond or free, and there was none to help Israel. [27] But the LORD had not said that he would blot out the name of Israel from under heaven, so he saved them by the hand of Jeroboam the son of Joash (*2 Kings* 14:23–27).

From these verses we are able to put together some parts of the jigsaw puzzle of Jonah's life. When we do so, the impression we are left with is that, living in admittedly dark and difficult days, Jonah was a man who enjoyed a number of invaluable spiritual privileges. In order to understand his flight from God, we will need to consider what these were.

## THE PRIVILEGE OF SERVICE

Jonah was God's servant (*2 Kings* 14:25). He was God's bond-slave, called to advance God's kingdom through obedience to his will. But the title 'servant' has a richer meaning even than this. Frequently it appears as a technical term in the Old Testament, for someone who has been specially set apart by God for a unique purpose. That is why the great figure of the Suffering Messiah who emerges from the shadows in Isaiah 52:13–53:12 is introduced by God as 'my servant'. In similar vein God speaks through Amos about 'his servants the prophets' (*Amos* 3:7). Those words underline for us the nature of Jonah's *privilege* as a prophet; for what Amos wrote was this:

> For the Lord GOD does nothing without revealing his secret
> to his servants the prophets.

Jonah belonged to that privileged band of men who had stood in the presence of God and felt the pressure of his will upon their spirits. They heard his unmistakable voice telling them what he was about to perform among the nations.

One of the Old Testament's words for a prophet is 'a seer'. He was a man who had insight, who 'saw' into the purposes of the eternal God, and was divinely commissioned to bring God's people under the practical authority of his Word. Jonah was a man of this order.

While we cannot say for certain whether the passage in 2 Kings refers to a period before or after Jonah's summons to Nineveh, it would more naturally seem to refer to Jonah's *earlier* ministry. If that is so, our picture of Jonah's privileges as God's servant is clarified. For these words suggest that his service was crowned with a measure of fruitfulness and success. People remembered what he preached. His message stuck in their minds and, more important, his prophecies were fulfilled. That was the chief test of whether a prophet was sent by God or not (cf. *Deut.* 13:1 ff.). And in the case of Jonah, history unfolded just as he said it would.

What an extraordinary privilege it must have been to be the mouthpiece of God in this way! But that was only the beginning of his spiritual inheritance.

## THE PRIVILEGE OF A SENSE OF DESTINY

In general terms 2 Kings 14 gives us sufficient information to identify the times in which Jonah lived. It was a time of crisis for God's people. Kings 'did what was evil in the sight of the

Lord' (*2 Kings* 14:24) with solemn consequences for the nation's
life. But those were also days in which God was at work. Jonah's
immediate predecessors in the prophetic ministry were Elijah and
Elisha. During their lifetime God had broken through the silence
of previous generations and was once again raising up his servants
to speak his Word with grace and power to the people. Against the
dark backcloth of sin and rebellion there stood out little glimmers
of light and hope. Jonah appears to have been one of this new
order of prophets called by God.

*It is characteristic of such men that they are deeply conscious of a sense
of destiny.* To be a true prophet of God, and to be made aware that
God has a destiny for one's life, were almost synonymous in the
thinking of the Old Testament. In every age those who have been
of service to God's kingdom, whether publicly or privately, known
or unknown, have been conscious of this sense of destiny. They
have devoted their lives to it.

We find the same consciousness in Paul. He recognized that he
was 'one untimely born' (*1 Cor.* 15:8). By nature he did not fit in to
the expected order of things. He was an apostle only because of the
special mercy of God in his life (*1 Tim.* 1:12–16). Over and over
again he insisted that it was God who had called him and set him
apart for his evangelistic and church-building ministries.

Naturally, such a sense of destiny is a burden. But it is also a
blessing. It safeguards us from falling to many temptations. Paul
again is an example. From the moment of his conversion God had
given him an inkling about the course of his future service (see *Acts*
26:16–18). He had been called by God to be an evangelist to the
Gentiles (see *Acts* 9:15; 22:15). But it was some time before this
took effect when, through the Holy Spirit, the church at Antioch
recognized that God was calling him to a very special ministry
(*Acts* 13:1 ff.). In later years, when Paul suffered as a prisoner, and
experienced hardship, he was wonderfully sustained by this sense

of destiny. He recognized that he was a prisoner 'on behalf of you Gentiles' (*Eph.* 3:1). *He knew what he was for!* That knowledge meant everything to him in times of darkness and stress.

*Few things are more important for the Christian than to have a conscious sense of God's destiny.* That destiny may not be one of spiritual fame. That is of secondary importance. What is important is that we have some sense of what we are *for*.

Joshua, the successor of Moses, had to learn this lesson the hard way. The narrative of the capture of Jericho is preceded by the strange story of Joshua's encounter with 'a man was standing before him with his drawn sword in his hand.' Joshua (naturally enough for the commander of Israel's massive numbers) asks: 'Are you for us, or for our adversaries?' (*Josh.* 5:13). The answer he receives is calculated to turn inside-out his whole way of thinking: 'No; but I am the commander of the army of the LORD. Now I have come.' Joshua fell to the ground in worship! The real question was not: Who was this strange figure for? It was: Who was Joshua for? Did Joshua grasp the true nature of his destiny? *Was he for the Lord?*

This knowledge ought to be one of the great motivating forces in our lives. It became that in Queen Esther's. Fearful to intercede for God's people although they faced possible annihilation, she was urged on to serve the Lord by Mordecai's penetrating words: 'And who knows whether you have not come to the kingdom *for such a time as this?*' (*Esther* 4:14). It was this question which drew from her lips the vow *to do what God had made her for:* 'and if I perish, I perish' (*Esther* 4:16).

The same kind of motivation sustained Nehemiah. Distracted on every hand, tempted to give up the work of rebuilding the walls of Jerusalem, he recognized what God had called him to Jerusalem *for*, 'I am doing a great work and I cannot come down. Why should the work stop while I leave it ?' (*Neh.* 6:3).

There appears to be a direct relationship between our usefulness in the service of God and the sense of destiny we have that, whatever happens, we are doing the work to which God has called us.

Jonah must have known something of this. He was God's man, God's servant, God's prophet. He had come to know God's will for his life. When we meet him in the opening words of the *Book of Jonah,* God is once more making it clear to him what he is *for.* That is a privilege beyond price!


## THE PRIVILEGE OF SPIRITUAL FELLOWSHIP

We naturally tend to think that these Old Testament prophets emerged from obscurity. Elijah, for example, strikes us as a kind of 'now you see me, now you don't' figure, as he appears and disappears with the message of God. One day, it seems, Amos is tending the flock, and the next day he is proclaiming God's Word (*Amos* 7:15). Consequently our natural inclination is to see the prophets as isolated stars in the sky, individuals and sometimes individualists (the melancholy Jeremiah, the eccentric Ezekiel).

*But God only appears to work suddenly.* In fact his movements across the scene of human history are well-planned, long-rehearsed, and constantly inter-related. That is why, whenever we think of Jonah's background, we ought to recall to mind a little phrase which is repeated in the early chapters of 2 Kings. Frequently in these chapters, set probably in the days of Jonah's teenage years, we find references to 'the sons of the prophets' (*2 Kings* 2:3, 5, 7, 15; 4:1, 38; 5:22; 6:1). These words give a hint of what God was doing. He was gathering around the prophets young men, devoted to his name, gifted in his service, and loyal to his servants. They served the prophets Elijah and Elisha, were exposed to their ministry of the Word of God, and bore a relation to them similar to that which Timothy bore to the Apostle Paul. They were trained for the advance of God's kingdom in these 'schools of the prophets'. Elisha in particular (himself a 'son' of Elijah) was a leading figure in this new movement of God's Spirit.

There is no way of knowing whether Jonah ever belonged to one of the 'schools of the prophets'. But he belonged to their generation. Indeed an old Jewish legend (and legend, alas it is!) affirms that Jonah was actually the son of the widow of Zarephath, and had been raised from the dead by Elijah for future ministry (*1 Kings* 17:7–24). It seems more than likely therefore that Jonah either was himself one of the 'sons of the prophets', or at least knew many of them. Under these circumstances, he would have made every effort to enjoy the tremendous spiritual encouragements of fellowship with like-minded young men (and women too! – see *2 Kings* 4:1).

Early years of spiritual fellowship invested in study, prayer, discussion, evangelism, and the sheer exhilaration of seeking to discover the will of God for our own lives, and the purpose of God for our fellowship, repay vast dividends in the future. Is there anything to be compared with the friendships forged then in the heat of fellowship? This comradeship lasts, and does not seem to be diminished by distance or by time. We ought to thank God with all our hearts if we have had the privilege of being bound together with fellow Christians like this, to live and to die for Christ and his cause.

*Three inestimable privileges:* Service, a Sense of Destiny, and Spiritual Fellowship. These form the background to the life of Jonah when we meet him in the opening verses of his book. This Jonah, to whom the Word of God now comes, is a man rich in spiritual blessings. His past life reads like a rare pedigree. But when we come upon him now, despite all his past privileges and usefulness, he is a man who slips, stumbles, and falls. The first lesson we learn is not so much the wonder of the privileges we may enjoy, but rather this solemn truth: *No past privilege, nor all past privileges together; no past obedience, nor fruitfulness in service, can ever substitute for present obedience to the Word of God.* Great blessings only bring present fruitfulness when they are met with continuing obedience.

When we first encounter Jonah, therefore, he is no longer the man he once was. The reasons will eventually unravel themselves as we read through his biography. But before we do so, we must recognize the practical importance, and indeed urgency, of directing these questions to ourselves: Am I living with only the memories of obedience in my life? Am I substituting my past spiritual record for the pressing responsibility of present submission to the will of God?

It is possible for men to say to Christ: 'Lord, Lord, did we not do many mighty works in your name?', but, through failure fully and wholeheartedly to serve him to the end, hear these words: 'I never knew you; depart from me' (*Matt.* 7:22–23). Past privileges and blessings serve then only to magnify the shame of our disobedience. How much we need to take to heart that it is one thing to begin, another to continue, and yet another to finish the course.

# 2

# ON THE RUN

*Now the word of the LORD came to Jonah the son of Amittai, saying,* <sup>2</sup> *'Arise, go to Nineveh, that great city, and call out against it, for their evil has come up before me.'* <sup>3</sup> *But Jonah rose to flee to Tarshish from the presence of the LORD. He went down to Joppa and found a ship going to Tarshish. So he paid the fare and went on board, to go with them to Tarshish, away from the presence of the LORD.* <sup>4</sup> *But the LORD hurled a great wind upon the sea, and there was a mighty tempest on the sea, so that the ship threatened to break up.* <sup>5</sup> *Then the mariners were afraid, and each cried out to his god. And they hurled the cargo that was in the ship into the sea to lighten it for them. But Jonah had gone down into the inner part of the ship and had lain down and was fast asleep.* <sup>6</sup> *So the captain came and said to him, 'What do you mean, you sleeper? Arise, call out to your god! Perhaps the god will give a thought to us, that we may not perish.'* <sup>7</sup> *And they said to one another, 'Come, let us cast lots, that we may know on whose account this evil has come upon us.' So they cast lots, and the lot fell on Jonah.* <sup>8</sup> *Then they said to him, 'Tell us on whose account this evil has come upon us. What is your occupation? And where do you come from? What is your country? And of what people are you?'* <sup>9</sup> *And he said to them, 'I am a Hebrew, and I fear the LORD, the God of heaven, who made the sea and the dry land.'* <sup>10</sup> *Then the men were exceedingly afraid and said to him, 'What is this that you have done!' For the men knew that he was fleeing from the presence of the* LORD, *because he had told them.* [11] *Then they said to him, 'What shall we do to you, that the sea may quiet down for us?' For the sea grew more and more tempestuous.* [12] *He said to them, 'Pick me up and hurl me into the sea; then the sea will quiet down for you, for I know it is because of me that this great tempest has come upon you.'* [13] *Nevertheless, the men rowed hard to get back to dry land, but they could not, for the sea grew more and more tempestuous against them.* [14] *Therefore they called out to the* LORD, *'O* LORD, *let us not perish for this man's life, and lay not on us innocent blood, for you, O* LORD, *have done as it pleased you.'* [15] *So they picked up Jonah and hurled him into the sea, and the sea ceased from its raging.* [16] *Then the men feared the* LORD *exceedingly, and they offered a sacrifice to the* LORD *and made vows.* [17] *And the* LORD *appointed a great fish to swallow up Jonah. And Jonah was in the belly of the fish three days and three nights* ( Jon. 1:1–17).

'Jonah rose to flee . . . from the presence of the LORD.' It is difficult to believe that this is the same man as the honoured servant of God whose blessings and privileges the previous chapter outlined. Yet we are not long on the Christian way before we discover that Jonah's flight from God is not merely an exaggerated drama from the pages of Scripture, but a harsh reality. The history of Christ's church bears eloquent testimony to the frequency with which such tragedies occur – yes, and greater tragedies than that of Jonah.

Off the east coast of Scotland, some miles down the Firth of Forth, there stands a rocky island known as the Bass Rock. It is celebrated largely for the notorious purpose to which it was put in the days of the Scottish Covenanters. There men were imprisoned for Christ and for seeking liberty in order to worship him.

But there is a cruel twist to the story. The Rock was purchased to be used as a prison by James Maitland, Earl of Lauderdale, for £4,000 (an 'exorbitant sum', as one chronicler records). This same James Maitland had once gone to London as a Commissioner of the Church of Scotland to take part in the composing of the *Westminster Confession of Faith*, the most famous expression of the very truths for which many of the 'Men of the Covenant' died. People spoke in later years of his 'change'. There can be little doubt, however the history of the period is to be interpreted, that Maitland 'rose to flee from the presence of the LORD' and the cost of following him. The spirit of Jonah did not disappear from the face of the earth in the belly of the great fish!

The same trends from time to time occur in our own Christian fellowship. To bring the matter nearer home, we see them clearly enough in our own hearts. The purpose of this section of Jonah's narrative is to share with us a practical analysis of how and why such turning from God takes place. Jonah provides us, rather after the fashion of David's confessions in Psalms 32 and 51, with an analysis of his disobedience. There appear to be two marks by which it is characterized:

## JONAH TURNED FROM GOD'S WORD

'*The word of the LORD came* to Jonah.' That is a common expression in the books of the prophets. It is used over one hundred times, and it indicates what it meant to be a prophet. It meant to be the recipient of a communication from God, a 'word' which contained a message. It meant to have a clear, fresh light shed upon oneself, or society, or the nations, by the living God. It meant to be drawn into God's presence to see things from his perspective.

The prophets often described the sharpness of such an encounter: it was a sword in their spirits, a burden on their shoulders, a hammer breaking their rocky hearts, a fire raging within them. It was bitter to taste. It *came*. It could not be halted, and it forced itself on them unbidden. It gripped their minds and touched their consciences. It impelled their emotions. They could not escape the certain assurance that the voice of God was sounding in their hearts and must now sound to others through their lips.

Noticing the way in which the word came to Jonah:

It came with great clarity: *Arise, go to Nineveh.*
It sounded a note of reality: *That great city.*
It gave him a heavy responsibility: *Call out against it.*

What then was Jonah's difficulty? It is perhaps easier to say what it was not. It was not an intellectual difficulty in the sense that he might have found this word from God difficult to understand. No, it was crystal clear.

There are times when spiritual problems and difficulties arise because of a failure to understand God's Word. Jesus underlines this in his parable about the various kinds of soils into which the seed of God's Word falls: 'When anyone hears the word of the kingdom *and does not understand it,* the evil one comes and snatches away what has been sown in his heart.' (*Matt.* 13:19). But patently this was not what happened in Jonah's experience; nor is it what usually happens in ours. It has been well said that our problem in obeying God is not that we do not understand what he is saying, but that we do!

When the word of the Lord came to Jonah, he did not need to go to his study to consult his commentaries and lexicons. God's word did not make him despair of understanding what the divine intention really was. No, his difficulty was not intellectual, and if the truth be told, ours is rarely if ever intellectual either.

Jonah's difficulty was moral. When God spoke to him on this occasion, about this particular matter, God's will and Jonah's came on to a collision course. Jonah had his own desires, plans, and ambitions to fulfil; Jonah had his own concepts of how things should be and how best he could serve God. The flesh made war on the Spirit (*Gal.* 5:17), and it seems that the flesh was victorious.

We might wonder whether God was deliberately shining the spotlight of his Word into an area of Jonah's life that had never been put to the test before, exposing a nerve, and then touching it to discover what response there might be. God's Word has a way of doing that kind of thing. It can divide between soul and spirit, joints and marrow, because it is sharper than any sword. Like an instrument which can detect microscopic differences, it can penetrate in our consciences between the limits of our willingness to obey and the point at which we may turn from God's commands (see *Heb.* 4:12-13).

In Jonah's case it was a long time before all this came out in the wash, and became plain. But what did his contemporaries make of it? Suddenly his life became a hive of activity. There he was going about the ordinary business of his ministry, and the next minute he was gathering his savings together and feverishly asking in Joppa's dockland whether anyone might be sailing that night. Perhaps his sudden flight was interpreted as a call to the mission field! Judging by our own hearts he might well have been able to cover over his innermost convictions and his clear disobedience by a flurry of activity. But activity is a poor substitute for obedience. Later on, when no more running was possible, he poured out the poison which had soured his spirit, in a 'last fling' against God as he sat outside the walls of penitent Nineveh:

> O LORD, is not this what I said when I was yet in my country? That is why I made haste to flee to Tarshish; for I knew that you are a gracious God and merciful, slow to anger

and abounding in steadfast love, and relenting from disaster
(*Jon.* 4:2).

What lay behind Jonah's rebellion? Nineveh was the capital city
of an enemy nation. In later years it would overrun the people of
God. Jonah had a sneaking suspicion that God might pardon it
(after all, he must already have preached about the grace and mercy
God would show to Israel, even in their sin). Where then would
Jonah's reputation be among his own folk? 'Traitor Prophet', they
would call him. More than this was involved, as we will discover,
but certainly not less than this. What Jonah found so deeply disturbing was that God was asking him to sacrifice his reputation
– and for the sake of these Ninevites, these 'Gentile dogs' who
deserved neither mercy nor grace from God or from Jonah! In
response he turned from God's word. It was more than he was
willing to bear, and the sharp edge of his love for his Lord and his
consecration to his service were blunted.

The desire to maintain a reputation among our fellows has
proved to be an insurmountable hurdle for many people. For some
it bars the way into the kingdom of God; for others it becomes
the rock on which their spiritual consecration is dashed. Perhaps
the words of the famous Alexander Whyte (author of the still-
published *Bible Characters*) convey the inner workings not only of
preachers like himself, but of many Christians:

> When I watch the working of my own heart . . . this is what I
> am compelled to write: I am Jonah. In the matter of my own
> reputation as a preacher that is. For I used to say, Let me die
> first before I am eclipsed by another in my pulpit and among
> my people. I fought with a Jonah-like fierceness against the
> remotest thought of my reputation ever passing over, in my
> day at any rate, to another.[1]

[1] *Bible Characters, Ahithophel to Nehemiah*, Edinburgh, n.d., p. 136.

The symptoms, admittedly, may differ. They often do. But the disease is the same. Often a Christian may run away from the Lord because God has asked him to 'lay in dust life's glory dead'. Do we not see this in our own hearts?

## JONAH TURNED FROM GOD'S PRESENCE

Two things go together:

i. 'Jonah rose to flee . . . from *the presence* of the LORD' (*Jon.* 1:3). Literally the words should be translated, 'Jonah rose to flee *from the face of* the LORD', as later in the same verse and again in verse 10.

ii. Jonah must have known that escape from God is ultimately impossible. He could not have been schooled by the great prophets and been ignorant of this foundation of all religion – that God is omnipresent. He knew too the confession of David:

O LORD, you have searched me and known me! ² You know when I sit down and when I rise up; you discern my thoughts from afar. ³ You search out my path and my lying down and are acquainted with all my ways. ⁴ Even before a word is on my tongue, behold, O LORD, you know it altogether. ⁵ You hem me in, behind and before, and lay your hand upon me. ⁶ Such knowledge is too wonderful for me; it is high; I cannot attain it. ⁷ Where shall I go from your Spirit? Or where shall I flee from your presence? ⁸ If I ascend to heaven, you are there! If I make my bed in Sheol, you are there! ⁹ If I take the wings of the morning and dwell in the uttermost parts of the sea, ¹⁰ even there your hand shall lead me, and your right hand shall hold me. ¹¹ If I say, 'Surely the darkness shall cover me, and the light about me be night', ¹² even the darkness is not dark to you; the night is bright as the day, for darkness is as light with you. O LORD, you have searched me and known me! (*Psa.* 139:1–12).

What then does Jonah mean by telling us that he ran from God's presence? He was not fleeing from his *omnipresence*. He was fleeing from his 'felt presence' (as our forefathers in the Christian faith used to say); from the God who had made himself known in grace and power. He was fleeing from the place of prayer, and service. He was fleeing from the sphere of evangelism to which God was calling him. In his panic he endeavoured to go as far away as he could from that spot on the map where God had written the name 'Jonah'. So he got on board a ship that was bound for Tarshish, probably what we know as Spain. Surely there he could push to the back of his mind the haunting pressures of that word from God which had spoken with such authority to his conscience: *Go to Nineveh!*

The rest of the story is well-known. As the ship sailed westwards across the Mediterranean, God pursued Jonah through winds and storms. At length Jonah confessed that the storm and danger were his responsibility, and he was thrown overboard, cast upon the mercy of God.

*Jonah's flight from God was at great cost.*

We are told that there was a literal price to pay (*Jon.* 1:3). Beyond that lay the fearful spiritual cost of his misadventure. We can picture this little prophet breathlessly counting out the coins for his ill-fated Mediterranean cruise, the adrenalin flowing as at last the ship weighs anchor and the port of Joppa disappears over the horizon. We can see him going below deck as the stars sparkle in the sky. He rolls over on his mat that night, exhausted with nervous tension, yet perhaps with an overwhelming sense of relief that the great decision has been taken. He has paid the fare. Perhaps it took his life-savings; but his last thought before sleep is: 'It was worth it!'

Yet, Jonah had 'paid the fare' in another sense. The God from whom he fled, Scripture tells us, is one in whose presence there is fullness of joy, and at his right hand are pleasures forevermore (*Psa.* 16:11). Jonah had forsaken *that* for *this:*

> Behold, the storm of the LORD! Wrath has gone forth, a whirling tempest; it will burst upon the head of the wicked (*Jer.* 23:19).

How could you, Jonah? But he did. And so do we.

*Jonah's flight was not without spiritual fruit.*

The extraordinary fact is that Jonah's sailing companions, these hardened sailors, were spiritually affected by his presence and God's dealings with him. When we meet these men, they are crying to their gods (*Jon.* 1:5). But we leave them offering a sacrifice to the Lord and making vows to serve him (*Jon.* 1:16). It is a very clear illustration of the principle that the fruitfulness of our lives for God is not itself a guarantee of the closeness of our lives to his will.

There are times in our lives when the Lord will employ us in his service despite our disobedience, to demonstrate that the grace, the fruit, and the glory are entirely his. Here indeed is evangelism and the sovereignty of God! But it is also a warning to us, lest we be deceived by what God is able to do into a false sense of fellowship with him. When we turn from God we will often snatch at any straw to justify our rebellion to ourselves. So wrote John Newton, in a perceptive letter 'On the Snares and Difficulties attending the Ministry of the Gospel':

> Beware, my friend, of mistaking the ready exercise of gifts for the exercise of grace. The minister may be assisted in public for the sake of his hearers; and there is something in the nature of our public work, when surrounded by a concourse of people, that is suited to draw forth the exertion of our abilities, and to engage our attention in outward services, when

the frame of the heart may be far from right in the sight of the Lord. When Moses smote the rock, the water followed; yet he spoke unadvisedly with his lips, and greatly displeased the Lord.[1]

No matter what our gifts are, we may find ourselves in Jonah's position. God uses us for his glory, and yet our hearts are not in tune with his. Beware of mistaking usefulness to God for communion with God!

*Jonah could find no way of escape.*

There never is a place where we are 'safe' away from God's presence, where we can be left, as we superficially say, 'in peace'. Martin Luther's comment is worth repeating:

Not only the ship, but the whole world becomes too small for Jonah . . . He finds no nook or corner in all of creation, not even in hell, where he might crawl in; but he must needs expose himself to the gaze of all creatures and stand before them in all his ignominy.[2]

So it must ever be with those who turn from God's Word, and run from his presence. *We cannot escape from God's presence, even if we will not live joyfully in it.*

---

[1] From a letter of Newton, 'On the Snares and Difficulties Attending the Ministry', in *The Works of John Newton* (1820; reprinted Edinburgh: Banner of Truth, 1985), vol. 1, p. 164.

[2] *Luther's Works*, vol. 19: *Lectures on the Minor Prophets II*, St Louis: Concordia, 1974, pp. 58, 65.

# 3

# THE CASTAWAY

*Now the word of the LORD came to Jonah the son of Amittai, saying, ² 'Arise, go to Nineveh, that great city, and call out against it, for their evil has come up before me.' ³ But Jonah rose to flee to Tarshish from the presence of the LORD. He went down to Joppa and found a ship going to Tarshish. So he paid the fare and went on board, to go with them to Tarshish, away from the presence of the LORD. ⁴ But the LORD hurled a great wind upon the sea, and there was a mighty tempest on the sea, so that the ship threatened to break up. ⁵ Then the mariners were afraid, and each cried out to his god. And they hurled the cargo that was in the ship into the sea to lighten it for them. But Jonah had gone down into the inner part of the ship and had lain down and was fast asleep. ⁶ So the captain came and said to him, 'What do you mean, you sleeper? Arise, call out to your god! Perhaps the god will give a thought to us, that we may not perish.' ⁷ And they said to one another, 'Come, let us cast lots, that we may know on whose account this evil has come upon us.' So they cast lots, and the lot fell on Jonah. ⁸ Then they said to him, 'Tell us on whose account this evil has come upon us. What is your occupation? And where do you come from? What is your country? And of what people are you?' ⁹ And he said to them, 'I am a Hebrew, and I fear the LORD, the God of heaven, who made the sea and the dry land.' ¹⁰ Then the men were exceedingly afraid and said to him, 'What is this that you have done!' For the men knew that he was fleeing from the presence of the LORD, because he had* *told them. <sup>11</sup> Then they said to him, 'What shall we do to you, that the sea may quiet down for us?' For the sea grew more and more tempestuous. <sup>12</sup> He said to them, 'Pick me up and hurl me into the sea; then the sea will quiet down for you, for I know it is because of me that this great tempest has come upon you.' <sup>13</sup> Nevertheless, the men rowed hard to get back to dry land, but they could not, for the sea grew more and more tempestuous against them. <sup>14</sup> Therefore they called out to the LORD, 'O LORD, let us not perish for this man's life, and lay not on us innocent blood, for you, O LORD, have done as it pleased you.' <sup>15</sup> So they picked up Jonah and hurled him into the sea, and the sea ceased from its raging. <sup>16</sup> Then the men feared the LORD exceedingly, and they offered a sacrifice to the LORD and made vows. <sup>17</sup> And the LORD appointed a great fish to swallow up Jonah. And Jonah was in the belly of the fish three days and three nights* (Jon. 1:1–17).*

Jonah had fled from his God. But there is no escape from God, and he was to discover what a fearful thing it is to fall into the hands of the living God (*Heb.* 10:31). But more than this, the narrative of Jonah's flight spells out in capital letters the spiritual disintegration that eventually characterizes disobedience. Before, his lifestyle had been held together by the principle of obedience to God's Word; his character had been transformed by constant recourse to God's presence. Now, with these two stable elements gone, Jonah appears as a man who is, spiritually, 'all at sea'. He had lost his moorings, and drifted out into the dangerous waters of backsliding from God.

This nautical metaphor is one which the Letter to the Hebrews employs for precisely the same spiritual condition in New Testament times. The author speaks about the grace of God and the marks of the presence of God which attended the ministry of the apostles (*Heb.* 2:1–4). He issues this warning:

Therefore we must pay much closer attention to what we have heard, lest we drift away from it.

The failure of the believer to hold fast to the Word of God eventually means that he drifts away from the Word, and also from the moorings of his whole life. A disintegration takes place.

What were the evidences of this in Jonah's life? He himself draws our attention to at least four of them:

## MISGUIDED BY CIRCUMSTANCES

'But Jonah rose to flee to Tarshish from the presence of the LORD. He went down to Joppa and found a ship going to Tarshish' (*Jon.* 1:3). He found exactly what he wanted!

What thoughts must have flashed through Jonah's mind at that moment? Was God being merciful to him, after all? Was this a sign from God, prospering him despite the niggling condemnation of his conscience? Did God in some ways sympathize with Jonah, and understand the very difficult position in which his servant was placed? Here at least was the prospect of several days on board ship, with time to think, to reason the matter through, to avoid foolishly and recklessly obeying the voice he had heard in his heart. After all, Jonah might well have thought, he could have been mistaken – perhaps God had not really called him to Nineveh. With such a frame of mind the provision of a berth on a boat to Tarshish was, perhaps, a gracious providence indeed. And so he went on board.

It did not prove to be a friendly providence, certainly not in the way Jonah might have hoped. Instead it brought him down to the very gates of death (*Jon.* 2:2, 6). The ship lying in the Joppa harbour was not meant to be a means of escape from God's clearly revealed word, but the most terrible instrument in the hands of God to bring his servant back to his senses. It was not God-given guidance at all; rather it was a severe test of Jonah in his wayward condition.

There is a much-needed spiritual lesson for us here. We live in days when experience is at a premium. Religious experience is also at a premium. At such times the church is always in danger of losing sight of the fact that God communicates his will fundamentally and primarily *through his revealed Word*. It is a mistake to look for God's guidance in more immediate and mystical ways – through subjective impressions on our spirits, through circumstances, through 'signs'. Jonah's error teaches us: *Do not be guided by providences when you are refusing to be guided by God's Word.* Do not take the events of your daily life as your instructor when you have not taken God's Word as a lamp to your feet and a light to your path (*Psa.* 119:105).

The consequences for Jonah were disastrous. They can be for us too. I well remember a young, well-educated man telling me about what he clearly regarded as a most remarkable series of providences. Indeed he was rejoicing in what he believed 'the Lord had done'. What he attributed to divine guidance was this sad story: he and a friend had gone on holiday together with their respective girl friends. By the time they returned (to cut a long story short) they were re-partnered; but not without a good deal of unhappiness in between. The 'guidance of the Lord' was evidenced in all this entirely by a series of 'coincidences'. I listened with an increasing sense of disquiet as the story unfolded, but found it impossible to persuade the young man of two basic things. *First,* that these events did not bear the ordinary marks of God's presence as the author of peace; and, *second,* that there were a number of elements in what had happened that ran counter to the wise counsel of Scripture to wait patiently for the Lord. He was not persuaded, and the former friendship we had known was dissolved. The cruellest stroke of all was later to hear of the path which the lives of these young people had taken. Spiritually, the providences they regarded as beneficent seemed to be the beginning of the end for them. As with the Israelites, God gave them what they wanted, but sent spiritual blight as its companion (*Psa.* 106:15).

C. H. Spurgeon once described a school friend who had a very violent temper. He would often flare up with anger. Invariably, Spurgeon recalled, he would throw something when he was angry. 'What struck me forcibly', he said, 'was not that he got angry; nor that he threw something when he was angry. But that whenever he was angry there was always something at hand to throw!' Does this not ring a bell with us? It is often true in the Christian pilgrimage. When we have a heart to rebel against God there will frequently be the providential means put before us to give us the opportunity. But when we are on the run from God, his providences are *wise tests*. They are never *gracious excuses*.

## POWERLESS IN A CRISIS

What was Jonah doing when the storm blew up and the tempest rocked the boat? He 'had gone down into the inner part of the ship and had lain down and was fast asleep' (*Jon.* 1:5). The Greek translation of the Old Testament, the Septuagint, suggests that the captain may only have found him because he was snoring! Certainly he was in a deep sleep, perhaps of sheer exhaustion, caused by the total dissipation of his energies in running away from God; perhaps in relaxation, now that he felt the crisis was over.

In earlier years in his ministry Jonah could never have dreamed that he would one day find himself in these circumstances, straying so far from God. He would naturally have thought that his God-given office, or his conscience (moulded these many years by God's word) would preserve him from such scandal. Surely these would never allow him really to stray? Backslide, he might; lose something of the early spiritual buoyancy, he could. But always, he knew in his heart of hearts, his conscience would clamour for a hearing if he began to go too near the spiritual danger zone. Then he would be drawn back to God in penitence and receive restoration and recommissioning.

But reality is so different from daydreaming. When the moment of crisis came, Jonah was in no condition to hear his conscience. His conscience, in turn, was in no condition to speak to him. He had silenced it. Now Jonah's ears heard no longer the word of God, or the voice of conscience, but the angry tones of nature, the storms and the tempests of heaven, accusing him of his guilt. Even then he had to be awakened by a pagan sailor before he could hear the accents of God.

The words with which Jonah was awakened are full of significance. In the Hebrew text they echo the words of God with which the book opens:

The word of the LORD came . . . Arise . . . call out . . . (*Jon.* 1:1–2).

The captain came and said . . . Arise, call out . . . (*Jon.* 1:6).

The words must have seemed to Jonah like a haunting echo from the past, exposing once more the guilt of his flight from God. Now God had sent this pagan to arouse him to his duties. If we do not keep 'short accounts' with God in our conscience, it will not be long before our once sensitive spirits will fail to respond to the touch of his hand, or the sound of his voice. So it proved to be with Jonah. It emerged in a sad fashion:

## ASHAMED OF HIS MINISTRY

Jonah rubbed the sleep out of his eyes and staggered on to the top deck, only to be met with a barrage of questions. The sailors had cast lots to see who was responsible before God for the calamity. The lot had fallen on Jonah (*Jon.* 1:7). So, they asked:

Who is responsible for this?
What is your occupation?
Where do you come from?
What is your country?
From what people are you?

The scene, despite opinions to the contrary, carries all the marks of authenticity. It has all the bizarre touches of the unlikely which often characterize such a crisis. Who would have time for such questions when the ship was going under? But such is the paradox of human experience. Bands play *Abide with me* when *Titanics* sink; men ask questions in storms when their consciences are awakened to the judgments of God.

Jonah answered the questions.

But there was one question which Jonah did not answer:

*What is your occupation?*

He confessed his liability; he owned his Hebrew nationality and his religion. Yet to this one question Jonah had no answer:

*What is your occupation?*

He was no longer able to say: 'I am a prophet of the LORD.' His witness had been silenced; the very work for which he had been created lay incomplete. He had no word from God to give!

It was, admittedly, a difficult situation. But it was not an impossible one. Some seven centuries later another ship with a prophet of God on board sailed across this same stretch of the Mediterranean, and encountered a similar storm. The danger was at least as great. But on this occasion the endangered ship carried a faithful servant who was sailing in obedience to the will of God. He was therefore discovering that the providences he encountered were his servants rather than his masters. He stood on deck, and announced: 'not a hair is to perish from the head of any of you.' In the midst of the storm he took food, and above the raging of the sea his voice could be heard giving thanks to God for his constant provision (*Acts* 27:34–35). Paul exercised a prophetic ministry, whereas Jonah forfeited his.

A fourth consequence of Jonah's backsliding was almost inevitable:

## HE DESPAIRED OF FUTURE USEFULNESS

'Pick me up and hurl me into the sea', he said (*Jon.* 1:12). There was nothing left for him now. He felt that God had no more use for him. He was no longer sure whether he was a true servant of God or not. But worse, he was no longer sure whether he was still a true child of God or not, for where there is no obedience there can be no assurance. He now felt both physically and spiritually, a castaway, with no guarantee of rescue, and the expectation of the reverse. Jonah's new-found friends, the sailors, did everything in their powers to alleviate the situation: 'The men rowed hard to get back to dry land, but they could not, for the sea grew more and more tempestuous against them' (*Jon.* 1:13). Like public executioners they begged pardon for the action they were now forced to take (*Jon.* 1:14). 'So they picked up Jonah and hurled him into the sea, and the sea ceased from its raging' (*Jon.* 1:15). It was a moment to touch the hearts of seafaring men. Inwardly they exclaimed, 'Even the winds and waves obey his God.' Outwardly they offered sacrifices, and made vows. But for Jonah they could do nothing. They could only commit him to the tender mercies of his God.

It would be to miss the point of this narrative if we did not pause, at least momentarily, to ask ourselves the question, 'Is something of Jonah reflected today in my own life?' Leader though I may be; minister, preacher, pastor, missionary, Christian worker, though I may be, have I turned from God's Word and presence? Have some of the effects of that already written their way into my biography?

Is God saying something to me through the dark providences of life? *Am I like Jonah?*

In the next chapters we will see what Jonah needed to do, and what we likewise need to do: how he cried to God for help; how he confessed his sin; how he looked for salvation; how he truly repented and trusted in God's grace. But you do not need to wait before seeking God like this. Your present need may be to seek his face now. If that is so, do not read on, but pray:

> O Jesus, full of truth and grace,
> More full of grace than I of sin,
> Yet once again I seek Thy face;
> Open Thine arms and take me in,
> And freely my backslidings heal,
> And love the faithless sinner still.
>
> Thou know'st the way to bring me back,
> My fallen spirit to restore:
> O for Thy truth and mercy's sake,
> Forgive, and bid me sin no more;
> The ruins of my soul repair,
> And make my heart a house of prayer.

Charles Wesley

# 4

# RETURN TICKET

*Then Jonah prayed to the LORD his God from the belly of the fish,*
*² saying, 'I called out to the LORD, out of my distress, and he*
*answered me; out of the belly of Sheol I cried, and you heard my voice.*
*³ For you cast me into the deep, into the heart of the seas, and the flood*
*surrounded me; all your waves and your billows passed over me.*
*⁴ Then I said, "I am driven away from your sight; Yet I shall again*
*look upon your holy temple." ⁵ The waters closed in over me to take my*
*life; the deep surrounded me; weeds were wrapped about my head*
*⁶ at the roots of the mountains. I went down to the land whose bars*
*closed upon me forever; yet you brought up my life from the pit, O*
*LORD my God. ⁷ When my life was fainting away, I remembered*
*the LORD, and my prayer came to you, into your holy temple. ⁸ Those*
*who pay regard to vain idols forsake their hope of steadfast love.*
*⁹ But I with the voice of thanksgiving will sacrifice to you; what I*
*have vowed I will pay. Salvation belongs to the LORD!' ¹⁰ And the*
*LORD spoke to the fish, and it vomited Jonah out upon the dry land*
( Jon. 2:1–10).

W e left Jonah drowning in the Mediterranean Sea.
The first section of his chronicle traced his sad
story against the background of his many spiritual privileges,
through his rebellion and disobedience, to the consequences of
his broken communion with God. It is a downward graph all
the way.

At this point we see again the extent to which the little Book of Jonah is about *evangelism and the sovereignty of God.*

Chapter 2 in the Hebrew text begins at Jonah 1:17 in the English translations. The great fish which swallowed Jonah in judgment was also sent by God to prepare him for the work of evangelizing Nineveh.

Jonah had been determined to run from God's will. We almost get the impression that he would have died rather than evangelize Nineveh! But God is determined that Nineveh will be evangelized. He has set his grace upon the Ninevites, and his heart beats with love and pity for them. Even more remarkably, God also intends that this out-of-step prophet will be his chosen instrument to bring the Ninevites to repentance. Jonah the Reluctant will be Jonah the Evangelist! It is significant that God has mercy upon his servant Jonah *before* Jonah witnesses the same God having mercy upon Nineveh.

Thus, as the second act in the drama begins, the God who had prepared inanimate nature by his sovereign will to speak to Jonah now prepares a great fish to be the instrument of his further dealings with the prophet's soul:

> And the LORD appointed a great fish to swallow up Jonah. And Jonah was in the belly of the fish three days and three nights.

It would be possible to give a good deal of attention to this marvel of the deep. It must be the most criticized fish that ever swam in the Mediterranean. One sometimes hopes that there may be provision made for fish to speak in the new earth, so that this poor creature can have the opportunity to answer its critics!

Various stories have been employed to vindicate the authenticity of the narrative. Among them is the remarkable record of a sailor who fell overboard, and was swallowed by a fish of similar proportions to the one mentioned in Jonah. But when a clear-thinking member of the crew fired a harpoon and struck the fish, the hapless sailor was vomited safely out, and rescued! Another tale recounts how a large fish was found dead on the shores of the sea, and when dissected was found to have swallowed a horse.

While it is commendable that we should carefully examine the authenticity of such tales, there are reasons for caution as we do so. The most important is, of course, that too much discussion about the great fish can divert us from the real issue. The narrative is not really about the fish at all. It has only a 'walk-on part' in this gripping drama. Focus on the great fish and we may lose sight of the great God.

If there is a natural miracle to wonder at here, it is essentially the miracle of Jonah's preservation over this extended period of time. But the deeper work of God took place, not in the belly of the fish but in the heart of the prophet; not in the realm of nature, but in the realm of grace. The book records a miracle characterized by restoration, not just by preservation.

Jonah himself recognized that a restorative work took place in his heart through this whole experience. He summarizes it in words reminiscent of David's in Psalm 18, when he was delivered from Saul:

I called out to the LORD, out of my distress, and he answered me (see *Psa.* 18:3, 6).

But this only sets the scene. For the clear and painful truth which emerges out of Jonah's supplication to God is this: Restoration to fellowship with God must begin in the very areas where rebellion formerly existed. That is what repentance basically involves.

In the Old Testament, repentance is denoted by a picture-word which means to return, to go back along the path on which you came. The great New Testament illustration is the Prodigal Son, painfully making his way back home along the very paths on which he had lightly skipped to the far country. Jonah, the Old Testament prodigal, must similarly return from his far country. Consequently two things were necessary for him.

## RETURNING TO THE PRESENCE OF GOD

Jonah prayed (*Jon.* 2:2). He is like the Psalmist:

> Out of the depths I cry to you, O LORD! O Lord, hear my voice! Let your ears be attentive to the voice of my pleas for mercy! If you, O LORD, should mark iniquities, O Lord, who could stand? (*Psa.* 130:1–3).

He is like the 'one afflicted' in Psalm 102, pouring out the poison in his soul in the presence of God, confessing how harshly he has thought of him. But the important thing is that *he is in God's presence;* he is praying. That is the mark of God's presence and his grace in a person's life.

The experience of Saul of Tarsus illustrates this vividly. When Ananias was encouraged by the Lord to go to the blinded Pharisee's aid to welcome him into the fellowship of Christ, he naturally protested: 'Not him, Lord. Not Saul the persecutor! I have heard of the harm he has already done, and the greater harm he intends to do to your people. How do I know that a work of grace has really been done in his life?' The answer was brief: 'Behold, he is praying' (*Acts* 9:11). So it was with Jonah. Whereas before he kicked against the pricks of conscience (which would have restrained him from his private persecution of God), and fled from God's presence (*Jon.* 1:3, 10), now he fled to God's presence (*Jon.* 2:4, 7).

In Jonah's case this took place dramatically. The intensity of the drama is indicative of the depths to which he had sunk in his sudden flight from the face of God, and the lengths to which God had to go to bring him back. But even Jonah's case must be seen in perspective. What is of primary importance is *that* he was restored, not *how* he was restored. God is able to use means to bring us back to himself which are as undramatic as these means were dramatic. He knows the way to bring us back. We must allow him to be the judge of what is necessary to restore us to his presence. What is important is that we should be brought back to live in the presence of God, and to know both the shame and the exhilaration of the restoration of grace.

This is a message not only for the individual Christian, but also for our corporate lives as believers, and especially for our communal meetings. Increasingly we need to be convinced that the most important thing in the world, in our personal lives, our evangelism, and our worship, is the presence of God. All other things are secondary and should serve this great end.

We should look for this in our worship. Our great need is for such a manifestation of the Lord's presence with us that strangers coming among us will find the secrets of their hearts exposed. Then they will fall down and confess the presence of Almighty God (*1 Cor.* 14:24–25). This is why Christ died, and why the Spirit is given; this is the goal of our salvation ultimately, that we might be presented before the presence of the glory of God (*Jude* 24). But God intends to make us conscious of his presence now as well as then, and he is prepared to go to any lengths to do so.

I remember that point being brought home to me with great force years ago in a conversation with a young man in the north of Scotland. He was weeping like a child. He had played Jonah in his life, turning his back on the clear voice of God. Then, within a short space of time, it seemed as if God had begun to demolish all his props and comforts, until he felt himself left with nothing. Martin Luther used to speak about God's 'merciful wrath', and this young man had tasted something of that order of things. But the memorable thing was not so much what God's hand seemed to have done, nor even his tears. The truly impressive thing was to see God's purpose accomplished in a broken and contrite spirit. The young man was back again in God's presence. Restored!

There is a second element we must recognize in Jonah's trauma:

## RETURNING TO THE WORD OF GOD

The second chapter of Jonah has a rather familiar ring about it. If we heard it read to us without its source being identified, we might wonder if it came from one of the Psalms. 'It sounds like Psalm 18, but then, parts of it sound like Psalm 42', we might well find ourselves saying. Any Bible with cross-references will bear out the strong similarity between this prayer and a number of the prayers of the Psalms. So close is the similarity that many scholars who reject the conservative view of the book of Jonah regard this chapter as a later compilation. Certainly, according to their view, it could never have been uttered by the prophet Jonah.

But in fact the psychological probability of Jonah praying exactly like this is very high indeed (leaving aside for the moment the more basic question of biblical inspiration). The phenomenon of a man of God utilizing the resources of the Psalms to enable him to approach God can be witnessed at almost any church prayer meeting.

The truth of the matter is that Jonah, who had formerly turned from God's living voice, had now returned to God's written Word. Elsewhere in Scripture the same pattern emerges:

My soul longs for your salvation; *I hope in your word* (*Psa.* 119:81).

I wait for the LORD, my soul waits, *and in his word I hope* (*Psa.* 130:5).

This is the sign of the genuine sonship of God's children in their hour of greatest need.

We have suggested that this is a general pattern. But there is also a structure to Jonah's experience which God had fashioned with him alone in mind. There was a special reason God held him under this terrible experience. Jonah needed to feel the grace of God towards himself before he would be a suitable minister of that grace to the people of Nineveh.

God had already tried to teach him this grace. The word he had brought to his own people was a word of grace. The hopeless despair of the pagan sailors should have made him cry out to God to show them his grace. The measure of 'grace' which the sailors had shown him in the storm should have shamed Jonah into longing for grace for all those who had never received it. But now the lesson was being taught 'for real'. *Now it was Jonah who needed grace.*

He felt barred from God's presence, as the Ninevites were soon to feel. He felt the absence of God, as they would also do. He was coming to see something of his own wretched condition and his spiritual bankruptcy, as they did. That was his supreme equipping for the task. God was fitting him uniquely for work in Nineveh.

The Lord delights to do this. He did it with Isaiah. He was called to preach both judgment and salvation, wrath and grace. He was to denounce the people's righteousness as filthy rags in God's sight. But what did he learn himself? That his own lips – the very instrument which God was to use – were unclean, and unfitted by sin for the service of God. To be a prophet to sinners, Isaiah had to learn his own sinfulness (*Isa.* 6:1–8).

We find the same thing with Paul. In his early letter to the Galatians, where he argues with such breathtaking power for the grace of God, he smites his opponents hip and thigh! (*Judg.* 15:8). But in later years we find the same apostle learning about grace in a way he confessed he had never really known before, when, in great pain, he discovered grace sufficient for all his needs and a strength which is perfected in weakness (*2 Cor.* 12:2–10).

God's teaching methods are perfect. Jonah was brought back into the path of God's presence from which he had slipped. He had to come back at the very point he left.

Think here of Simon Peter, perhaps the greatest New Testament illustration of what we might call the 'Jonah principle'. He too was brought back to Christ at the very point of his departure. After the resurrection he was drawn near to a fire of burning coals, reminiscent of the earlier fire which had cost him his loyalty to Christ; three times his heart was smitten and broken open by a question, framed to convict him of sin and to cleanse him from it. Once it had been: *'Do you know him?'* Now it was *'Do you love him?'* The issue was the same. Like Jonah the way down was rapid. He fled from Christ's word, and he fled from his presence. But he was arrested by his providence. Like Jonah, too, he was brought back to Christ's word, for he 'remembered the word the Lord had spoken' (*Luke* 22:61, NIV). Like Jonah 'he went out and wept bitterly' (*Luke* 22:62). But he wept his way back to the presence of God.

The story of Jonah finds many echoes in the pages of Scripture. It finds many more in the pages of history. Does it find an echo in your own heart too? Then here are your priorities: Return to God's Word; return to God's presence:

Seek the Lord while he may be found; call upon him while he is near; let the wicked forsake his way, and the unrighteous man his thoughts; let him return to the Lord, that he may have compassion on him, and to our God, for he will abundantly pardon (*Isa.* 55:6–7).

# 5

# MERCIFUL WRATH

*Then Jonah prayed to the* LORD *his God from the belly of the fish,*
*² saying, 'I called out to the* LORD, *out of my distress, and he*
*answered me; out of the belly of Sheol I cried, and you heard my voice.*
*³ For you cast me into the deep, into the heart of the seas, and the flood*
*surrounded me; all your waves and your billows passed over me.*
*⁴ Then I said, "I am driven away from your sight; Yet I shall again*
*look upon your holy temple." ⁵ The waters closed in over me to take my*
*life; the deep surrounded me; weeds were wrapped about my head*
*⁶ at the roots of the mountains. I went down to the land whose bars*
*closed upon me forever; yet you brought up my life from the pit, O*
LORD *my God. ⁷ When my life was fainting away, I remembered*
*the* LORD, *and my prayer came to you, into your holy temple. ⁸ Those*
*who pay regard to vain idols forsake their hope of steadfast love.*
*⁹ But I with the voice of thanksgiving will sacrifice to you; what I*
*have vowed I will pay. Salvation belongs to the* LORD!' *¹⁰ And the*
LORD *spoke to the fish, and it vomited Jonah out upon the dry land*
(Jon. 2:1–10).

'Before I was afflicted I went astray, but now I keep your word'
(*Psa.* 119:67) might well be written over this segment of
Jonah's experience. The great instrument God had used to work a
spirit of repentance in his servant was the suffering of being cast
into the Mediterranean Sea and being entombed in the belly of the

great fish. There, as we saw in general terms, Jonah began to hold on to what he knew of God's written Word and to seek God's face in prayer.

But, in Jonah's case, the work of grace had to plough very deeply into his soul. His confused thinking about God and his ways needed to be focused, the blunt edge of his spiritual experience needed to be sharpened. Jonah had become insensitive to the presence of God, and there were a number of things that he needed to recognize. As he continued in prayer, the truth about himself and his situation began to dawn upon him.

## AFFLICTION FROM GOD'S HAND

Chapters 1 and 2 provide some interesting comparisons. The difference in Jonah is immediately striking. But they can also be compared, as history compares with prophecy. While history interprets events from the human point of view, prophecy sees them from God's viewpoint. Back in chapter 1:15, Jonah had narrated the bare facts of the story: So *they picked up Jonah* and hurled him into the sea. But in chapter 2:3 the perspective of reawakened faith appears: '*You cast me* into the deep', he says to God.

In theological language Jonah is reflecting on the difference between secondary and primary causes. In spiritual terms he is experiencing what every awakened person feels: the sense that God's presence is so real and near that each event in life is seen to be under his control.

Jonah knew well that God controlled everything. It would not have been news to him to learn that God rules the sea (he told the sailors that *his* God had made the sea – see *Jon.* 1:9). But the voice that speaks in chapter 2 is the voice of the awakened backslider, not the voice of the trained theologian. When God begins to work in us like this, we learn to understand the words (which, interestingly, meant a great deal to Martin Luther and John

Calvin), 'I will make their hearts so fearful . . . that the sound of a wind-blown leaf will put them to flight' (*Lev.* 26:36, NIV).

When we are aroused from spiritual lethargy, we become conscious of the weight of God's judgment; we recognize that we are in the presence of a holy God and yet have lived without a thought for his majesty. Every circumstance of life seems to be enlarged in its significance by his all-pervasive presence. We come to appreciate not only 'the sovereignty of God', but God, the Living Sovereign himself. So it was with Jonah. He came to see that 'from him and through him and to him are all things' (*Rom.* 11:36).

The experience could have been put down simply to misfortune – the misfortune of being accidentally found out. A matter of coincidence! It was a tragedy – although he was lucky to escape! *But Jonah could never, ever see it that way.* That can never be the perspective of the man with an awakened conscience which is sensitive to the very touch of God when he draws near. He must say: 'This is the finger of God' (see *Exod.* 8:19).

Few principles are more important in the Christian life than the practical recognition of the sovereign God, and his gracious determination to draw us near to himself, whatever the cost may be. When his purposes involve afflictions and suffering of any kind, the knowledge that he is sovereignly over-ruling is the only thing that can preserve us from a craven fear or a sense of despair, and bring us a measure of joyful and willing acceptance of our situation. Only when we recognize that God's aim is to make us like Christ (cf. *Rom.* 8:29), and that he works all the events of our lives together for this purpose, will we begin to rejoice in the good that is produced out of tribulation (*Rom.* 5:3–5). Joni Eareckson Tada illustrates the point movingly:

> I really don't mind the inconvenience of being paralysed if my
> faithfulness to God while in this wheel chair will bring glory

to him . . . When God brings suffering into your life as a Christian, be it mild or drastic, he is forcing you to decide on issues you have been avoiding. He is pressing you to ask yourself some questions: Am I going to continue trying to live in two worlds, obeying Christ and my own sinful desires? Or am I going to refuse to worry? Am I going to be grateful in trials? Am I going to abandon my sins? In short, am I going to be like Christ? He provides the suffering, but the choice is yours.

But today as I look back, I am convinced that the whole ordeal of my paralysis was inspired by his love. I wasn't a rat in a maze. I wasn't the brunt of some cruel divine joke. God had reasons behind my suffering, and learning some of them has made all the difference in the world.[1]

There is a note of biblical authenticity about words like that from a young quadriplegic. It is this note of authenticity which sounds through the confession of Job, and brings him to the place of joyful recognition of the hand of God which others, like Joni Eareckson Tada, have discovered:

I know that you can do all things, and that no purpose of yours can be thwarted . . . I had heard of you by the hearing of the ear, but now my eye sees you; therefore I despise myself, and repent in dust and ashes (*Job* 42:2, 5–6).

No wonder Jonathan Edwards, the eighteenth-century New England theologian and preacher so mightily used by God, wrote that he found the most gracious work of God was generally performed when he was preaching on the sovereign Lord. When God is seen and sensed as the living Lord he really is, then the groundwork is laid in our lives for true spiritual restoration.

[1] *A Step Further* (Grand Rapids, 1978), pp. 42, 77, and 14.

But the hand of God stretched out in naked sovereignty can be a terrifying sight. It cannot be viewed on its own without damage being done to our spiritual vision. That is why Jonah needed to see more than divine sovereignty.

## CHASTISEMENT FOR JONAH'S SIN

When Jonah cried to the Lord from the belly of the great fish, he did so not merely as a subject craving a hearing with his Sovereign, *but as a child conscious of the chastisement of his Father*. The rod with which his back had been bruised was not being wielded in an arbitrary fashion. Its main function in fact was not really punitive at all, but restorative and disciplinary. How does this emerge in the passage itself? It does so in three ways:

1. In verses 5–6, Jonah seems to speak of the last judgment of God on his life:

> The waters closed in over me to take my life; the deep surrounded me; weeds were wrapped about my head at the roots of the mountains. I went down to the land whose bars closed upon me forever.

Yet, he is able to confess:

> Yet you brought up my life from the pit, O LORD my God.

Not only so, but in verse 4 he calls upon God with a sense of hope. There is some problem about the translation of these words, as a comparison of ESV and AV or NIV will show. The best rendering would seem to be this:

> I said, 'I have been banished from your sight; Yet I will look again towards your holy temple.'

In other words, at the heart of his trials, when the tunnel through which he is passing seems to be unendingly gloomy, Jonah begins to see light and hope. Most of all he realizes that his experience has had a *purpose*. That is the difference between condemnation and chastisement.

2. A second reason for believing he learned this fresh perspective lies in the change which took place in his own thinking. At first he was concerned only about being *cast down* (*Jon.* 2:3), but under the hand of God he became more concerned about the fact that he had been *cast out from the presence of the Lord;* 'Then I said, "I am driven away from your sight"' (*Jon.* 2:4). That, again, is always the mark of the man or woman who begins to recognize the hand of a Father behind the circumstances of life. Whereas we were concerned mainly about our physical condition and our material needs, now our relationship to God is all that really matters.

3. Jonah also shows the characteristic responses of a man under the chastising hand of God. Proverbs 3:11–12 and Hebrews 12:5–6 describe them in the form of an exhortation:

> My son, do not regard lightly the discipline of the Lord, nor be weary when reproved by him. For the Lord disciplines the one he loves.

In the opening chapter we came upon Jonah despising the disciplines of the Lord; in chapter 2, by and large, the despair with which the previous chapter concluded is expressed in many phrases of his prayer. Like a pendulum he was swinging from one extreme response to the other, *until he saw his Father's hand.* Then he realized that, however painful such discipline was for the present, afterwards it would yield the peaceful fruit of righteousness through its training (*Heb.* 12:11). Jonah was learning the lesson which John Bunyan expressed so well in his epigram:

> Thou art beaten that thou mayest be better.

Jonah recognized *the sovereign hand of God,* and *the fatherly chastisement of God.* But there is a third element in his restoration which was essential to it.


## GRACE IN GOD'S HEART

The pattern which begins to emerge in God's dealings with his recalcitrant servant is quite exquisite:

His sin had cast him down ('To the roots of the mountains I sank down', NIV)

but

God brought him up ('You brought up my life from the pit')

His sin had cast him out ('I am driven away from your sight')

but

God brought him in ('My prayer came to you, into your holy temple').

God took Jonah (like the Psalmist before him) from the pit, and released his feet from the mud and mire. He set his feet on a rock, gave him a firm place on which to stand, and put a new song in his mouth (*Psa.* 40:2). From the deepest hell he had been taken to heaven itself and the presence of God. In a profound sense he was discovering: 'If I make my bed in Sheol, you are there' (*Psa.* 139:8).

By the time Jonah's prayer draws to an end we find that he is a changed man. God has touched his life and become real to him in a new way. There is a freshness about his communion that is different from anything we have seen in his life thus far.

In fact, God graciously effected a number of things in Jonah:

1. *Grace produced a new sense of compassion.*

When we turn from the Lord in the way Jonah did, we inevitably turn away also from a true perspective on the lives of our fellow-men. We close our hearts towards them.

Imagine Jonah being rudely awakened by the sea-captain in chapter 1, turning over on his mat and thinking to himself: 'Who does this Gentile dog think he is?' What we have discovered about the prophet's heart suggests that when he saw these pagan sailors calling upon their deaf gods, he must have despised them. 'Salvation comes from the Jews', he might well have thought, 'and salvation ends with the Jews.'

But in the depths of his own need he had seen how compassionate God had been to him, and now, instead of sitting in judgment *over* these pagans, he now sat beside them, *under* God's judgment. He began to have compassion on them. He saw them as Christ was later to see the multitudes, as 'sheep without a shepherd', and he confessed 'Those who pay regard to vain idols forsake their hope of steadfast love' (NIV: 'forfeit the grace that could be theirs', *Jon.* 2:8). Jonah who had formerly despised the ungodly heart had now seen God's judgments on his own ungodly heart, and learned compassion. Now that he too had felt despair and known what it is to be far from God, the Ninevites must have appeared to him in a new light. They were no longer a heathen enemy, but immortal men under God's judgment, and in need of hearing his warning voice.

The church today, and many of us as individuals, desperately need to learn this lesson. If grace does not make us like Christ in his compassion for men and women and young people who have never heard the gospel, then it is no more grace. How perverse Jonah was! Living in a favoured nation where spiritual light had shone only because of the great mercy of God, he had come to assume that Israel deserved grace, whereas others had ill-deserved it. What a perversion! Yet it lies like a hidden poison in the hearts of some of us who most fervently profess evangelical convictions. It is an unwritten rule in our hearts – others do not deserve the gospel, so why should we exhaust our lives taking it to them?

Alas, when we think like that we show how little we know of our own need, how little we feel the judgment of God on our own lives, how little we really know of the grace of God! Shame on us! We should tremble when we read of the seriousness with which God took such an attitude in his servant Jonah, and when we see the severity with which he exposed and healed it.

2. *Grace produced a new sense of consecration.*

'What I have vowed I will pay', says Jonah. 'I with the voice of thanksgiving will sacrifice to you' (*Jon.* 2:9). Apparently Jonah has not been *brought forward* to a higher degree of consecration, but *brought back* to an earlier level of commitment. This 'new sense of consecration' takes him back in his memory to some significant event, or period in his life. At that time – was it in the belly of the fish, or years before, when he first became aware of the call to be a prophet? – he had made a solemn vow to the Lord. In the belly of the fish, were Jonah's thoughts many miles away, and several years in the past – as though it were yesterday? Did he see himself as a young man bowing down in prayer before God, and yielding himself to his service in such terms as these?

> Lord, speak to me, that I may speak
> In living echoes of Thy tone;
> As Thou hast sought, so let me seek
> Thy erring children lost and lone.
>
> O strengthen me, that while I stand
> Firm on the rock, and strong in Thee,
> I may stretch out a loving hand
> To wrestlers with the troubled sea.

O use me, Lord, use even me,
Just as Thou wilt, and when, and where,
Until Thy blessed face I see,
Thy rest, Thy joy, Thy glory share.

Frances Ridley Havergal

Now, he found himself praying the same prayer again.

As we look out on a world so much of which remains unevangel-ized, should we not be sharing in his prayer of re-consecration?

3. *Grace produced a new sense of God.*

'Salvation belongs to the Lord', Jonah declared (*Jon.* 2:9). In itself, an innocent enough remark, and altogether orthodox in its theology. But now it was charged with the meaning gained from personal experience. He could hardly have failed to have given this same testimony before; certainly not if he had any acquaint-ance with the great prophet Elisha whose very name meant '*God* is Saviour'! But in the dark no-man's land where Jonah had been, this had begun to take on a new meaning, or at least had come home to him with new power.

Writers in the past used to make a distinction, between *the knowledge of the truth* and *the knowledge of the power of the truth.* That was exactly the distinction Jonah had learned. He had already known these truths about God, and obviously in some way had experienced God at work in his life. But now he had come to know God. In the darkness the light had dawned that the ultimate truth about God was not that he was Israel's God, or Jonah's God; nor was it that he was a God who had spoken to the fathers. The ultimate truth about God, which he now felt so mightily in his own soul, was that *God is a saving God.* When Jonah learned that, he was ready to go to Nineveh. Now he was ready for the word of the Lord to come to him 'a second time' (*Jon.* 3:1). If there was salvation for Jonah, might there not also be salvation for Nineveh? So, God spoke to the fish, and it vomited Jonah on to the dry land. He shook himself, and began the trek from wherever he had come ashore to the great city of Nineveh.

Before we visit Nineveh with him, however, we ought to pause to see the path on which he has come; to marvel at the lengths to which God is prepared to go for his children, and the efforts he is willing to make for them. He will go to any lengths to bring us into the centre of his will, no matter what the price may be, either to him or to us. Few things in Christian experience are more wonderful than this, and few things more awesome.

C. S. Lewis depicts the costly joy of our dealings with God, and his with us, in *The Lion, the Witch and the Wardrobe*. The youngsters who have chanced into the world of Narnia, a land cursed by the White Witch so that it is 'always winter, but never Christmas', hear of the promised saviour-king of the land, Aslan. Enquiring further they discover from Mr Beaver that he is a lion:

> 'Ooh!' said Susan 'I'd thought he was a man. Is he – quite safe? I shall feel rather nervous about meeting a lion.'

> 'That you will, dearie, and no mistake', said Mrs Beaver, 'if there's anyone who can appear before Aslan without their knees knocking, they're either braver than most or else just silly.'

> 'Then, he isn't safe?' said Lucy.

> 'Safe', said Mr Beaver. 'Don't you hear what Mrs Beaver tells you? Who said anything about safe? 'Course he isn't safe. But he's good. He's the King, I tell you.'[1]

---

[1] *The Lion, the Witch and the Wardrobe* (1950; New York: Harper Collins, 1978), pp. 79–80.

Jonah discovered something similar. Life could never be 'safe' as a servant of the living God, certainly not as a runaway servant. But,

> Good and upright is the LORD; therefore he instructs sinners in the way (*Psa.* 25:8).

Jonah would have been able to confess, now, at last, with another Psalmist:

> I know, O LORD, that your rules are righteous, and that in faithfulness you have afflicted me. Let your steadfast love comfort me according to your promise to your servant (*Psa.* 119:75–76).

Is that our confession too?

> Other refuge have I none;
> Hangs my helpless soul on Thee;
> Leave, ah! leave me not alone;
> Still support and comfort me,
> All my trust on Thee is stayed;
> All my help from Thee I bring;
> Cover my defenceless head
> With the shadow of Thy wing.
>
> CHARLES WESLEY

# 6

# THE SIGN OF JONAH

*Then the word of the LORD came to Jonah the second time, saying,
² 'Arise, go to Nineveh, that great city, and call out against it the
message that I tell you.' ³ So Jonah arose and went to Nineveh,
according to the word of the LORD. Now Nineveh was an exceedingly great city, three days' journey in breadth. ⁴ Jonah began
to go into the city, going a day's journey. And he called out, 'Yet
forty days, and Nineveh shall be overthrown!' ⁵ And the people of
Nineveh believed God. They called for a fast and put on sackcloth,
from the greatest of them to the least of them. ⁶ The word reached the
king of Nineveh, and he arose from his throne, removed his robe,
covered himself with sackcloth, and sat in ashes. ⁷ And he
issued a proclamation and published through Nineveh, 'By the
decree of the king and his nobles: Let neither man nor beast,
herd nor flock, taste anything. Let them not feed or drink
water, ⁸ but let man and beast be covered with sackcloth,
and let them call out mightily to God. Let everyone turn from
his evil way and from the violence that is in his hands. ⁹ Who
knows? God may turn and relent and turn from his fierce
anger, so that we may not perish.' ¹⁰ When God saw what they
did, how they turned from their evil way, God relented of the
disaster that he had said he would do to them, and he did not do it*
(Jon. 3:1–10).

W e know nothing about that moment in Jonah's life when he rubbed his eyes and stretched out his hand to make sure that he really was on dry land. The previous thirty-six hours must have seemed like an eternity to him. The nightmare encounter with the storm, and the contacts with the sailors – they would seem so vivid in his memory, and yet his own experience of God's power since then had been so profound, so life-shattering, they must have seemed like the events of a previous year. He was certainly a wiser, and hopefully, a better man than he had been merely hours before. To this changed man 'The word of the LORD came . . . the second time' (*Jon.* 3:1).

Jonah's experience was unique. But its inner principles are often seen in the lives of God's children. There are many Christians who confess that it is only because 'the word of the LORD came the second time' to them that they are now engaged in serving the Lord. When God called first of all, he met with reluctance, diffidence, perhaps even selfish ambition and plain stubbornness. In this sense most of us are 'Jonah'.

It is solely because we have a God of persistent grace that we are serving him today. But, as we noticed in Jonah's case, God is determined that his servants will serve him, no matter what it costs him, and no matter what it may cost them! God does not deal with us in half-measures. He is committed to us 'up to the hilt' as it were, and the thoroughness of his commitment to us is the measure of the lengths to which he will go to make us fruitful and faithful children. He does not give up on his designs for our lives.

Unless we are reading the Book of Jonah for the first time, we are already a jump ahead of him. He did not know what would happen if he went to Nineveh (although he seems to have had more than a suspicion about it, see *Jon.* 4:2). But we do know. We realize that he is being sent by God to be the human instrument in a mighty revival and a national repentance which will bring salvation to the people of Nineveh. It is precisely at this point that another strand in the pattern of God's dealings with him begins to emerge. For God's purpose is this:

*The salvation of one Hebrew sinner*

is intended to produce:

*The salvation of many Ninevite sinners.*

It was the restoration of Jonah which was the means of the revival in Nineveh. This is a great illustration of what we might call equipping grace and evangelistic grace.

## EQUIPPING GRACE

The apostle Paul indicates that the inspired Word of God has the function of 'kitting out' the Christian for his service (*2 Tim.* 3:16–17). It has power to influence and change him.

God's Word does this *in its own strength,* even when we ourselves are reluctant to be obedient to it. It has power to break down our disobedience and to bring us to a new level of submissiveness. This certainly happened with Jonah. Despite his initial disobedience to God's word of command, Jonah was being shaped by it. A moment's reflection on what would have happened if Jonah had immediately gone to Nineveh will confirm this to us. *What would have happened?* Perhaps very little!

Jonah was not really fitted to be the evangelist of the Ninevites. He had no comprehension of their condition, nor had he any true sympathy for them. He did not share the compassion of Christ who would have gathered Jerusalem sinners to himself as a mother hen gathers her young. Jonah would have died rather than pray for the Ninevites: 'Father, forgive them, for they know not what they do' (*Luke* 23:34). He needed to be broken, melted, moulded, and filled with the love of God for the lost before he would be of any use to

God in this field of service. *But that could not happen without Jonah's disobedience and flight from God.* It is clear, however mysterious it may seem, that God used even the result of Jonah's disobedience to equip him for service. God had apparently taken that into account already. He had not only expected it, but he was going to employ the consequences of it for his own glory. That does not excuse Jonah's disobedience. Nor did God act towards Jonah as though he treated his disobedience as a matter of indifference.

We would be foolish to think that anything God ever says or does means that we can treat sin lightly. But, when his children return to him in true evangelical repentance, accepting his chastisements and humbling themselves before him, they should hang on firmly to the knowledge that God is able to make his name a praise among the nations even on the shoulders of his children's failures and sins. Nothing will stop him. If need be he will use the devil himself (as indeed he ultimately will) to bring glory to his name, and to fit his own people for their temporary and eternal destinies.

The principle by which God works is that where sin abounds grace super-abounds (*Rom.* 5:20). It is this super-abundance of grace and wisdom in God which can make our experiences, even in rebellion against him, serviceable in his hands to equip us for the future. Broken and contrite-hearted Jonah was precisely the kind of man God could use in Nineveh.

There is a word here for us all – all except those who would turn this grace of God into an *excuse* for their disobedience (*Rom.* 6:1; *Jude* 4). We may have turned from God's will. God may have dealt with us severely. We may have felt there is no hope for us. But if we are his children this principle stands inviolable:

> And we know that for those who love God all things work together for good, for those who are called according to his purpose (*Rom.* 8:28).

'All things' must mean *every* thing, or it means *nothing*. Yes, even sin. God is as great as this in his grace. He works in our lives so that we may be ready for that moment when the word of the LORD comes a second time.

## EVANGELISTIC GRACE

If the principle behind Jonah's restoration is God's overarching *sovereign grace,* then the principle which lies behind the events which were to follow in Nineveh was this: God intends to bring life out of death. We may well think of this as the principle of all evangelism. Indeed, we may even call it 'the Jonah principle', as Jesus seems to have done. It is vital to our understanding of the fundamental principle of this little book that we try to follow this whole matter through.

In the Gospels, Jesus replied to the demands of the Pharisees for an authenticating, convincing sign, in these words: 'An evil and adulterous generation seeks for a sign, but no sign will be given to it except the sign of the prophet Jonah' (*Matt.* 12:39–40; 16:4; *Luke* 11:29–30). He went on to explain that just as Jonah was in the belly of the fish for three days and nights, so the Son of Man would be in the heart of the earth. What lies behind this enigmatic saying? Simply the truth that it is out of Christ's *weakness* that the sufficiency of his saving *power* will be born. It is out of his *death* that men will receive *life*. The same principle is expressed in John's Gospel (significantly, when Gentiles asked to speak with Jesus):

> Truly, truly, I say to you, unless a grain of wheat falls into the earth and dies, it remains alone; but if it dies, it bears much fruit (*John* 12:24).

Fruitful evangelism is the result of this *death-producing-life* principle. It is when we come to share spiritually – and on occasions physically – in Christ's death (cf. *Phil.* 3:10) that his power is demonstrated in our weakness, and others are drawn to him. This is exactly what was happening to Jonah. Christ had not yet come. But there was a sense in which, through faith in his promised appearance, Jonah was sharing in the fruit of Christ's death working in his life, forgiving and cleansing him, and empowering him for service.

The apostle Paul recognized this, and expounded it at length to the Corinthians:

> We are . . . always carrying in the body the death of Jesus, so that the life of Jesus may also be manifested in our bodies. For we who live are always being given over to death for Jesus' sake, so that the life of Jesus also may be manifested in our mortal flesh. So *death is at work in us, but life in you* (*2 Cor.* 4:8, 10–12).

Scripture expresses the same thing through many pictures. Like a mother experiencing agonizing labour pains, the apostle Paul was willing to suffer in order that Christ might be fully formed in his converts (*Gal.* 4:19). It is those who go out *weeping* with their precious seed who will return with *rejoicing* (*Psa.* 126:6). It is the man who has been *emptied* of himself who will be *filled* with Christ. Here we stand at the heart of the principle of spiritual fruitfulness:

> There is no gain but by a loss:
> You cannot save but by a cross.
> The corn of wheat, to multiply,
> Must fall into the ground and die.
> Wherever you ripe fields behold,
> Waving to God their sheaves of gold,
> Be sure some corn of wheat has died,
> Some soul has there been crucified;
> Someone has wrestled, wept and prayed,
> And fought hell's legions undismayed.

In the sovereign purposes of God there was revival in Nineveh. The instrument of that revival was Jonah. He was by no means perfect. He had many elements of remaining sin clearly visible in his life, clinging to him as tightly as the seaweed he pulled from his body as the sun rose over him on a Mediterranean beach. But something had happened to him. Something in him had been slain by the grace of God. It was out of Jonah's inner death that life was born in Nineveh.

Ought we not to be prepared likewise to die – for the life of others? Is it because we refuse to die that we 'abide alone'? God help us to die, that we may bear much fruit and so prove to be Christ's disciples! Only then will the sign of Jonah be seen in the church of Christ.

# 7

# SPREADING THE WORD

*Then the word of the LORD came to Jonah the second time, saying, ² 'Arise, go to Nineveh, that great city, and call out against it the message that I tell you.' ³ So Jonah arose and went to Nineveh, according to the word of the LORD. Now Nineveh was an exceedingly great city, three days' journey in breadth. ⁴ Jonah began to go into the city, going a day's journey. And he called out, 'Yet forty days, and Nineveh shall be overthrown!' ⁵ And the people of Nineveh believed God. They called for a fast and put on sackcloth, from the greatest of them to the least of them. ⁶ The word reached the king of Nineveh, and he arose from his throne, removed his robe, covered himself with sackcloth, and sat in ashes. ⁷ And he issued a proclamation and published through Nineveh, 'By the decree of the king and his nobles: Let neither man nor beast, herd nor flock, taste anything. Let them not feed or drink water, ⁸ but let man and beast be covered with sackcloth, and let them call out mightily to God. Let everyone turn from his evil way and from the violence that is in his hands. ⁹ Who knows? God may turn and relent and turn from his fierce anger, so that we may not perish.' ¹⁰ When God saw what they did, how they turned from their evil way, God relented of the disaster that he had said he would do to them, and he did not do it* (Jon. 3:1–10).

God was dealing with Jonah as a father would with his erring child. He had allowed him to choose his own way long enough to feel the misery of it. He had chastened him to imprint the necessary lessons in his memory. In one sense he had broken the spirit of rebellion in Jonah so that he could never be the same again. But now he was acting once more like a father, as he took Jonah aside and said to him, in essence: 'Go to Nineveh now, *and this time do what I tell you!*'

It may not be insignificant (although commentators seem to ignore the point) that the Lord says something slightly different to Jonah this time. The *first time* he had said:

Arise, go to Nineveh, that great city, and *call out against it,* for their evil has come up before me (*Jon.* 1:2).

The *second time* the message was in these terms:

Arise, go to Nineveh, that great city, and *call out against it the message that I tell you* (*Jon.* 3:2).

In the first instance a clear message was given to him; in the second a clear command to render total obedience, *whatever the message might be.*

So the story proceeds. Jonah went to Nineveh. It was a large city – 'three days' journey in breadth' (*Jon.* 3:3). But Jonah had scarcely seen one third of its streets and marketplaces before God seemed to take hold of him and Nineveh through him, and shake them both to the roots of their beings. It does not seem that language proved to be a great barrier to communication. Jonah exclaimed: '*Yet forty days, and Nineveh shall be overthrown!*'

A mighty awakening took place among the inhabitants. The remainder of the chapter describes how the people came before God in repentance and faith. From the king on the throne to the beasts in the field, Nineveh was filled with a spirit of penitence.

At this point many scholars raise an objection once again to the whole idea that Jonah is an historical narrative. 'How', they ask, 'can a revival have possibly taken place in Nineveh when we find no record of it, and within a few generations the Ninevites had overrun the people of God?' If a revival had taken place, they argue, it would be quite impossible for these later events to have taken place.

This is a serious objection. But it is one that lacks spiritual and historical perspective. Take the United Kingdom; take Wales, or Northern Ireland, or Scotland. Within a similar period of time these small countries have witnessed remarkable revivals of religion, with no less remarkable occurrences than in Nineveh. But it is not long before these are but memories of the past. Within a few generations little is remembered within communities once visited by the power of God.

People who experience mighty revivals may be all the more hardened against God in the generations that follow. The presence of the Spirit of God is a far more delicate matter than we are prone to imagine. We need have no hesitation in believing that a revival of the magnitude described in Jonah chapter 3 really took place in Nineveh.

*We stand in need today of such a revival and awakening.* Nothing short of this would seem to leave any hope that the multitudes of men and women outside of our churches will ever hear and respond to the gospel. If we do not believe that, a bus ride through the massive housing estates in any of our great cities should soon convince us. They are full of those who, spiritually, 'do not know their right hand from their left' (*Jon.* 4:11). If a preacher were to wander for three days through these areas, what would he find? He might begin to feel what G. K. Chesterton called 'the sense of the absence of God'. God is not in men's thoughts (*Psa.* 10:4). Many have never heard of Christ; they do not go to a place of worship; they have never really been invited to one. They may never have met and spoken to an unashamed Christian. There are so few of us making any effort whatsoever to communicate with them. There would seem to be no hope of them being won for Christ unless God penetrates these rows of homes, and his presence reverberates in the hearts of the multitudes. That, after all, is essentially what happens in a revival. God is sensed!

Revival often comes when the church begins to take this situation with seriousness; when, like Jonah, it is awakened to the needs of men and women who do not know God.

This was brought home to me in the most poignant circumstances while visiting an elder in our congregation. He was a fine Christian man whose life God had most wonderfully touched. But he was in a cancer ward. As we talked and shared fellowship together he gestured towards the far end of the ward. There, on opposite sides were two boys not yet in their teens. One wore a Glasgow Rangers soccer jersey, the other sported the green and white hoops of their arch rivals Glasgow Celtic.

The boys' beds were decorated with the trappings of fervent supporters, and the evidence that perhaps one or two members of these famous Scottish clubs had come to visit them. If so, it must have been one of the most difficult and moving experiences of their lives. For these boys were in my friend's ward for the same reason he was. 'Do you see those two lads?' he asked. 'I discovered that they had never heard of Jesus.'

I drove home feeling as never before the failure of the church's witness, and the great need to cry to God to come down and touch the hearts of people in sovereign mercy. How much we need a revival – as much as Nineveh did!

But it is vital to recognize that Jonah was not sent to Nineveh with the assurance of being a 'revivalist'. He was sent there as an evangelist. He was commissioned by God as a herald. He was to fulfil the role of a witness – 'Proclaim . . . the message I give you'

(*Jon.* 3:2, NIV). Revival is needed, and we must pray for it. But evangelism is the divine command, and we must be obedient to it. It is essential therefore that we try to learn something from Jonah's proclamation of the Word of God.

What were the salient features of the testimony which Jonah brought to the people of Nineveh?

## SIMPLICITY AND CLARITY

That is the first thing to strike us about the narrative. Jonah proclaimed:

*Yet forty days, and Nineveh shall be overthrown!*

Was that all he said? It may well have been. Alternatively these words may be only a summary of a message he brought to them at greater length, arguing his case and bringing forward reasons for his conviction that the judgment of God was upon the city of Nineveh. Perhaps he confessed the supernatural circumstances which had brought him to them. But whether this is a verbatim quote or a greatly abbreviated summary of Jonah's witness to Nineveh, in either case the message was direct, simple, and clear. Even if he spoke at great length, there could be no doubt about what he was saying.

This is a tremendously important thing for Christians today to recognize in the spreading of the Word of God. How readily we confuse people by our hobby-horses; like the Emperor Nero we fiddle while Rome burns. How little we feel the burden of the Word of the Lord, so that its weight is concentrated on fundamental matters.

Our God-given task is simply and directly to teach God's Word and truth to our contemporaries. God may use us and our testimony as he pleases, but we have a responsibility to make his truth as clear as we are able. So often it is our own lack of clear thinking, or a weak grasp of the Word that makes our witness confused and sometimes confusing. It lacks thrust because it lacks a concentration of our energies in presenting the great basics of the gospel. To say this is not to make a plea for superficiality, nor is it to downgrade the importance of a thorough grounding in all the doctrines of the Bible. In fact it is the reverse, for a really thorough grasp of biblical teaching and the relation between its doctrines will always help us to put the weight of our testimony where it really belongs.

Inevitably this has a special application to preachers and teachers of the Word. Paul speaks about this in an important section of 2 Corinthians. He writes:

> But we have renounced disgraceful, underhanded ways. We refuse to practise cunning or to tamper with God's word, but by the open statement of the truth we would commend ourselves to everyone's conscience in the sight of God (*2 Cor.* 4:2).

'The open statement of the truth' is the essence of the privilege of explaining the Scriptures to others. It involves seeing to the heart of God's Word, and bringing out its truth simply and clearly. It means seeing to the heart of the listener and applying the truth to his life in a way that demonstrates both his own need and God's perfect grace to save and help him.

Jonah learned this lesson from God himself. God had spoken to him with the same simplicity and directness. But how slow he had been to receive and apply the lesson!

## THE POWER OF GOD

It is very evident from the effects of Jonah's preaching that God turned his words into arrows which pierced the consciences of his hearers. 'The people of Nineveh believed God' (*Jon.* 3:5), runs the record. Of course, it follows that they must have believed Jonah, but they did not feel that it was the voice of Jonah they heard.

Through him, and behind him, they recognised the voice of the living God.

This is the mark of what is often called *'unction'*. It is that special 'coming' or 'filling' of the Spirit of God which makes the Word of God run from the heart of the preacher to those of the hearers. 'I had the wind behind me, and we were travelling downhill', as someone once described his experience of preaching. Perhaps it has never been better expressed than by E. M. Bounds in his unique little book *Power Through Prayer:*

Unction is that indefinable, indescribable something which an old, renowned Scotch preacher describes thus: 'There is sometimes somewhat in preaching that cannot be described either to matter or expression, and cannot be described what it is, or from whence it cometh, but with a sweet violence it pierceth into the heart and affections and comes immediately from the Lord.' We call it unction. It is this unction which makes the Word of God 'quick and powerful, and sharper than any two-edged sword, piercing even to the dividing asunder of soul and spirit, and of the joints and marrow, and a discerner of the thoughts and intents of the heart.' It is this unction which gives the words of the preacher such point, sharpness, and power, and which creates such friction and stir in many a dead congregation. The same truths have been told in the strictness of the letter, smooth as human oil could make them; but no signs of life, not a pulse throb; all as peaceful as the grave and as dead. The same preacher in the meanwhile receives a baptism of this unction, the divine *inflatus* is on him, the letter of the Word has been embellished and fired by this mysterious power, and the throbbings of life begin – life which receives or life which resists. The unction pervades and convicts the conscience and breaks the heart.

This divine unction is the feature which separates and distinguishes true gospel preaching from all other methods of presenting the truth, and which creates a wide spiritual chasm between the preacher who has it and the one who has it not. It supports and impregnates revealed truth with all the energy of God. Unction is simply putting God in his own Word and on his own preacher. By mighty and great prayerfulness and by continual prayerfulness, it is all potential and personal to the preacher; it inspires and clarifies his intellect, gives insight and grasp and projecting power; it gives to the preacher heart power, which is greater than head power; and tenderness, purity, force flow from the heart by it. Enlargement, freedom, fullness of thought, directness and simplicity of utterance are the fruits of this unction . . . What of unction? It is the indefinable in preaching which makes it preaching. It is that which distinguishes and separates preaching from all mere human addresses. *It is the divine in preaching* (*Power Through Prayer*, Chapter 15).

This is our great need! Those who preach and teach need it, and Christians have a corporate responsibility to pray for anointed preaching and teaching (cf. *Eph.* 6:19–20; *2 Thess.* 3:1). But we also need to look to God for this anointing on our own personal witness, even upon the few sentences which we may speak for Christ to others. This was the secret of the spread of the gospel in the days of the apostles. According to the Acts, 'they were all filled with the Holy Spirit and continued to speak the word of God with boldness' (*Acts* 4:31). When God's anointing is on our witness, eloquence of speech is no advantage; the ability to speak only a few sentences is no hurdle to the Holy Spirit.

J. Edwin Orr records a moving illustration of this in his documentation of *The Second Evangelical Awakening*. Speaking of the revival in Northern Ireland in 1859, he says:

The townsfolk of Coleraine, in the part of County Derry close to the County Antrim Revival centres, witnessed some of the most amazing scenes in the whole movement in Ireland. A schoolboy, under deep conviction of sin, seemed so incapable of continuing his studies that the kindly teacher sent him home in the company of another boy, already converted. On the way home the two boys noticed an empty house and entered it to pray. At last the unhappy boy found peace, and returned immediately to the classroom to tell his teacher: 'I am so happy: I have the Lord Jesus in my heart!' This innocent testimony had its effect on the class, and boy after boy slipped outside. The master, standing on something to look out of the window, observed the boys kneeling in prayer around the schoolyard, each one apart. The master was overcome, so he asked the converted schoolboy to comfort them. Soon the whole school was in strange disorder, and the clergymen were sent for and remained all day dealing with seekers after peace, schoolboys, schoolgirls, teachers and parents and neighbours, the premises being thus occupied until eleven o'clock that night.

On 7 June 1859 an open-air meeting was held on Fair Hill to hear one or two of the converts. So many thousands attended that it was deemed advisable to divide the crowd into separate meetings, each addressed by an evangelical minister of one denomination or another. The people stood motionless until the very last moment, when an auditor cried in distress. Several others likewise became prostrated, bewildering the ministers, who having had no similar experience previously, scarce knew how to help the distressed in soul and body. The clergymen spent all night in spiritual ministrations, and when the sun arose, the following day was spent in like manner.

*The Second Evangelical Awakening,* pp. 48–49.

It must have seemed to observers as if Jonah had returned from the dead. One sentence, anointed by the Spirit of God – and Coleraine was awakened!

The history of revivals is punctuated by such narratives. But a moment of quiet reflection on our own experience may suggest that most *individual* conversions also begin in this way *with a few words that God takes and uses to arrest us*. It may be something in a sermon, of course. But it is as likely, perhaps more likely today, to be some few stumbling words of witness by a Christian we know. The *way* it was said, the *time* at which it was said, *our own spiritual condition* when we heard it – God used all of these to bring us into his kingdom.

When I was almost fifteen years old I began to realize, in a way I had never done before, that I stood in need of salvation. One winter evening as I walked home I slid in the snow beside a small, elderly man. Under the dim light of the street-lamp I could see that he was dressed entirely in black! After a moment's conversation, he asked, 'Son, are you saved?' The words were like a knife in my soul. How did the man know that it was my greatest longing in life to know that I was a child of God? By these and other words God guided me into his kingdom. I often looked for the man thereafter, to tell him that God had anointed his words. But he never seemed to walk that road, at that time of night, again. I learned then that sentences are all God needs when his children have the touch of the Spirit on their lives. What hope and confidence this inspires in our witness!

So, in this confidence Jonah walked through the streets of Nineveh with his message. We may well imagine (and later discover) that there were imperfections in his preaching. But he spoke with direct application to his hearers. He brought to Nineveh the message he felt *Nineveh* needed to hear. He had been prepared for such a ministry, because when God had risen up as a witness to him, God had spoken to Jonah the word that Jonah needed to hear. In his grace he had also spoken to Jonah the word that Nineveh would later hear. He had prepared him for the task. Jonah had now, at last, discovered:

> That word can only come with power to our hearers when it has come with power to our own hearts.
>
> JOHN OWEN

# 8

# NINEVEH AWAKENED

*Then the word of the LORD came to Jonah the second time, saying,*
*² 'Arise, go to Nineveh, that great city, and call out against it the*
*message that I tell you.' ³ So Jonah arose and went to Nineveh,*
*according to the word of the LORD. Now Nineveh was an exceed-*
*ingly great city, three days' journey in breadth. ⁴ Jonah began*
*to go into the city, going a day's journey. And he called out, 'Yet*
*forty days, and Nineveh shall be overthrown!' ⁵ And the people of*
*Nineveh believed God. They called for a fast and put on sackcloth,*
*from the greatest of them to the least of them. ⁶ The word reached the*
*king of Nineveh, and he arose from his throne, removed his robe,*
*covered himself with sackcloth, and sat in ashes. ⁷ And he*
*issued a proclamation and published through Nineveh, 'By the*
*decree of the king and his nobles: Let neither man nor beast,*
*herd nor flock, taste anything. Let them not feed or drink*
*water, ⁸ but let man and beast be covered with sackcloth, and*
*let them call out mightily to God. Let everyone turn from his*
*evil way and from the violence that is in his hands. ⁹ Who*
*knows? God may turn and relent and turn from his fierce*
*anger, so that we may not perish.' ¹⁰ When God saw what they*
*did, how they turned from their evil way, God relented of the*
*disaster that he had said he would do to them, and he did not do*
*it (Jon. 3:1-10).*

The womenfolk who gathered for their morning chat at the Nineveh well could scarcely have guessed what lay on the heart of the stranger they watched making his way to the city gate on the morning of the revival. Little did they know that they would themselves lay their heads on tear-stained and prayer-saturated pillows before the sun rose over the well on the following morning, and they gathered again, this time clothed in sackcloth.

What happens in a revival? From one point of view it is simply the magnifying and multiplying of what happens whenever God breaks suddenly into our lives.

One of the great values of studying revival in a biblical account such as this is that it puts under the microscope for us the fundamental elements of all genuine spiritual experience. It places in sharper focus what happens when God's Word begins to search our hearts and touch our wills. It magnifies for us what we should always expect to happen through the anointed witnessing and preaching we considered in chapter 7. Jonah chapter 3 encourages us to pray for revival; it also describes the perennial effects of the working of God's Spirit through the Word. Four of these effects deserve special consideration.

## ILLUMINATION

When there is 'the open statement of the truth' (*2 Cor.* 4:2) our minds are illuminated in a new way. This was what happened in Nineveh. The citizens woke up one morning assuming that all was more or less the same as it always had been. They did not have the spiritual awareness to sense that the cloud of divine judgment was stretched across the city already. The god of this world had blinded their minds (*2 Cor.* 4:4). They were unconcerned because they had a mistaken interpretation of their situation. Suddenly, through Jonah's words, they found a flood of light shining into their hearts with alarming power. They no longer stood at the bar of human justice; they could not think about this little prophet merely in natural terms; they saw the divine judgment over their heads, and they began to cry out to God for mercy. A total reversal took place in their thinking! Instead of complacency and indifference, their hearts were stirred to pray 'God be merciful to me, a sinner' (*Luke* 18:13).

Jesus teaches us that this is the work of the Holy Spirit. It is he who calls us in question before God's judgment seat, and awakens us to the true state of our hearts. We find ourselves convinced and convicted of our sin – just as men were on the Day of Pentecost (see *John* 16:8–11 and *Acts* 2:37).

In the case of Nineveh, the ministry of Jonah was exactly the same as that exercised by Paul: he had been sent to *open the eyes of the Gentiles* (*Acts* 26:17–18). Only that painful, powerful light of God's truth would bring them to their senses and to repentance.

Such illumination is glorious, but it can be frightening. It exposes the needs in our hearts and the sin in our lives that we never knew existed. But it is also glorious, because the light which falls can bring comfort and healing to us. God, in his infinite knowledge and perfect wisdom, not only touches our inmost being, but he also unravels his grace, pours in the medicinal balm of his love, and points us in the way we should go. He penetrates through the soul and the spirit. In a widespread way, and on a massive scale, this took place in Nineveh. It continues to take place through the ministry of God's Word. That is why the Psalmist prayed:

> Send out your light and your truth; let them lead me; let them bring me to your holy hill and to your dwelling! Then I will go to the altar of God, to God my exceeding joy, and I will praise you with the lyre, O God, my God (*Psa.* 43:3–4).

## CONVICTION

'The people of Nineveh believed God', reported Jonah (*Jon.* 3:5). There are times in days of revival when people believe preachers rather than God, respond in a great wave of enthusiasm, and return to their old godlessness almost as quickly. There seems to have been an element of this in the revival which swept through Samaria under the preaching of Philip the Evangelist (*Acts* 8:4–13, specially verses 6, 12–13). But the Ninevites, at least in the generality, recognizsed God's own voice coming through Jonah's words. They were stopped in their tracks.

They were convicted and convinced. But of what? Primarily of their spiritual danger. It was certainly of their danger that Jonah had warned them. He had preached to them the message of God's law: 'You have sinned and rebelled against God; you have fallen under the curse of God; you are under the wrath of God; rouse yourselves to the present danger!' It is a great tragedy when this note is no longer sounded by Christians today. It needs to be recovered, because it is a note that runs through all the preaching of the Bible, from Moses and the prophets through John the Baptist, our Lord Jesus himself, to the apostles – Paul and John and Peter. Nor should we be deceived into thinking that to speak of the prospect of judgment is to be lacking in love. To believe so is to cast moral criticism on the character of Jesus himself (cf. *Matt.* 23–25). Furthermore, to warn men of the judgment to come is the only course that biblically instructed love can take.

Our home used to be on one of the small islands in Shetland. Down one side of the island ran spectacular cliffs where birds gathered in their hundreds. Often tourists came to watch them. Sometimes, however, a major tragedy occurred. Walking along the cliffs, some visitors failed to notice where the grass suddenly stopped and the cliff began. There was no natural warning. One step might be on solid ground, but the next – over the cliff face. If a local person saw a visitor go too near the edge, would he be melodramatic, or lugubrious, to shout out a warning? On the contrary, it would be the only loving thing to do.

That was how Jonah felt. He had recently been on the other side of the precipice. He had returned as a warning sign to the Ninevites. But if they went over the spiritual precipice on which they stood, there would be no way back. In the same way, to have become a Christian is, in some measure, to have come to realize our danger, to have been convinced of it for ourselves. It is to come under an obligation to warn others also, and to do everything within our powers to rescue them from the verge of spiritual disaster. It is unlikely that others will be convinced of their danger if we are not convinced of it.

## SPIRITUAL MOURNING

The people declared a fast and put on sackcloth. The king rose from his throne and sat down in the dust. Together they called urgently upon God. They became truly sorry for what had happened; they mourned because they did not know the blessing of the presence of God with them. They longed for a change of lifestyle, and the opportunity to demonstrate that they were in earnest about it as they gave up their evil ways and their violence (*Jon.* 3:8). This used to be called *compunction*. Their consciences were stabbed, and they began to have scruples about their previous easy-going disobedience to God and indifference to his presence and glory. They experienced what the Corinthians later did:

> You felt a godly grief ... For godly grief produces a repentance that leads to salvation without regret, whereas worldly grief produces death. For see what earnestness this godly grief has produced in you, but also what eagerness to clear yourselves,

what indignation, what fear, what longing, what zeal, what punishment! (*2 Cor.* 7:9–11).

We are bound to recognize that if some degree of this is not brought home to our hearts through God's Word, then little deep and lasting work is likely to be done there.

## FAITH AND REPENTANCE

The fruit of Jonah's witness to Nineveh was that the people turned from their wicked ways. That is repentance – not only regretting sin, but abandoning it. But it is clear from the context in Jonah 3 that this repentance was not isolated from the accompanying exercise of faith.

There is a tendency for Christians to assume that repentance is experienced before faith, and leads to faith. But this view is due to a misunderstanding. It tends to confuse conviction with conversion, mourning for sin with turning away from sin, which is the hallmark of repentance. Furthermore, the real repentance which brings life accompanies faith rather than causes it. The penitence of the Ninevites expressed this 'mustard seed' of faith in God:

Who knows? God may turn and relent and turn from his fierce anger, so that we may not perish (*Jon.* 3:9).

This was not mature faith, or strong faith, or the full assurance of faith by any manner of means. But it was faith nonetheless. It had grasped something about Jonah's God even when the message appeared to be one of unmitigated gloom: *he was a God who might have mercy.* Trusting in his gracious character, they pled with God that he might be merciful to them. They were not his people; they were strangers to the covenant and the promises (see *Rom.* 9:4; *Eph.* 2:11–13), but they hoped that the God who had sent this Jewish preacher might be a God of love as well as a God of holiness. They threw themselves helplessly on his character. Like the woman from Syrian Phoenicia, they called upon the Lord: 'Even the dogs under the table eat the children's crumbs' (*Mark* 7:28). Might there be crumbs of grace in God for penitent Ninevites?

We find this combination of believing repentance and penitent faith throughout Scripture. There is forgiveness with God that he may be feared (*Psa.* 130:4). The biblical combination is necessary if we are to have a healthy spiritual experience and a well-focused understanding of the God with whom we have to do. We dare not approach him without repentance for sin; but we become morbid if we fail to reach out to his grace. Jonah himself had been brought to repentance by divine warning, but only because he found in God a divine welcome for penitents. So it was with the Ninevites.

The last verse of chapter 3 records God's gracious response:

> When God saw what they did, how they turned from their evil way, God relented of the disaster that he had said he would do to them, and he did not do it.

Nineveh had been saved! Revival had come! Repentance had been born.

Before we turn to a very different scene in Jonah's life, we should remind ourselves again of the great principles which were at work in this divine visitation. God had begun to work in Jonah that he might work through Jonah. That was not a guarantee of revival in Nineveh, but it was part of its explanation, just as the emptying and inner crucifying of Simon Peter is part of the explanation of the mighty outpouring of the Spirit which took place in Jerusalem on the Day of Pentecost. God worked sovereignly then in his evangelism, as in Nineveh. But he longed to use human instruments, and to do so they had to be hand-made, custom-built for his glorious purposes. The jewels of spiritual service are always quarried in the depths of spiritual experience. Never is this more true than in revival. That is the significance of the motto of one of the Welsh revivals: *Bend the church and save the people.*

Will we be bent, and broken for God's service? Will the sin of Jonah in our hearts become the sign of Jonah? Only when the sign of Jonah is seen in the church will the power of God be seen in the world.

# 9

# AT LOGGERHEADS

*But it displeased Jonah exceedingly, and he was angry. ² And he prayed to the LORD and said, 'O LORD, is not this what I said when I was yet in my country? That is why I made haste to flee to Tarshish; for I knew that you are a gracious God and merciful, slow to anger and abounding in steadfast love, and relenting from disaster. ³ Therefore now, O LORD, please take my life from me, for it is better for me to die than to live.' ⁴ And the LORD said, 'Do you do well to be angry?' ⁵ Jonah went out of the city and sat to the east of the city and made a booth for himself there. He sat under it in the shade, till he should see what would become of the city. ⁶ Now the LORD God appointed a plant and made it come up over Jonah, that it might be a shade over his head, to save him from his discomfort. So Jonah was exceedingly glad because of the plant. ⁷ But when dawn came up the next day, God appointed a worm that attacked the plant, so that it withered. ⁸ When the sun rose, God appointed a scorching east wind, and the sun beat down on the head of Jonah so that he was faint. And he asked that he might die and said, 'It is better for me to die than to live.' ⁹ But God said to Jonah, 'Do you do well to be angry for the plant?' And he said, 'Yes, I do well to be angry, angry enough to die.' ¹⁰ And the LORD said, 'You pity the plant, for which you did not labour, nor did you make it grow, which came into being in a night and perished in a night.*

*<sup></sup>¹¹ And should not I pity Nineveh, that great city, in which there are more than 120,000 persons who do not know their right hand from their left, and also much cattle?' (Jon. 4:1–11).*

I have met men who would give their right arms to see what Jonah saw in Nineveh, for whom the privilege of being an instrument of awakening in the hands of God would be sweeter than life itself.

From any viewpoint it was a time of unusual grace. The circumstances that brought Jonah to the city, the unction that attended his preaching, the penitent faith of the citizens – all these are indications of the day of mercy that dawned in Nineveh. It was a story to which our Lord Jesus Christ could point back and say: 'The men of Nineveh will rise up at the judgment with this generation and condemn it, for they repented at the preaching of Jonah' (*Matt.* 12:41; *Luke* 11:32). It was in fact a kind of foretaste of the Day of Pentecost, when once again God would grant 'repentance that leads to life' to the peoples of the Gentile world (cf. *Acts* 2:5–12; 11:17–18). There are many Christians today who long for a time when God's servants need to go only a day's journey until there is a large response to the Word of God. How many would sacrifice everything to have seen those revival days in Nineveh! What would we do if a Day of National Repentance were declared in our own land or if the leaders of the nation clothed themselves in garments of repentance and began to cry to God?

But we now discover that the final chapter of Jonah is perhaps the most puzzling and mysterious of all. It almost seems like the prototype of our modern dramas in which, instead of everything turning out right in the end, things seem to fall apart and we are left feeling disturbed and uneasy. When the zoom lens focus on Jonah moves away from him to take in the panorama of Nineveh repenting in the background, the caption reads: 'Should not I pity Nineveh, Jonah?', and we take our leave of the prophet, once again under divine cross-examination. It is enigmatic. It rocks us back on our heels and contradicts all that we might have expected.

The more familiar we become with Jonah, and with what we see of Jonah in our own hearts, the more reluctant we will be to tie up the many loose ends of the book. This closing chapter seems enigmatic simply because Jonah *is* an enigma. He is a contradiction of himself. *But life is full of contradictions.* This particular story, which is so true to the paradoxes and contradictions of life is worth summarizsing in this chapter so that we may catch the 'feel' of the situation.

After preaching, Jonah witnessed the scenes of repentance, engaged in prayer, and withdrew from the city. The heart of the significance of the chapter lies in the contrast between God's response to Nineveh's repentance and Jonah's response to it:

When God saw what they did . . . *God relented* (*Jon.* 3:10, see also 4:2).

When Jonah saw what God did *he was displeased exceedingly and angry* (*Jon.* 4:1).

Whereas God was slow to anger (*Jon.* 4:2), Jonah was immediately angry.

What did Jonah do in his anger? He prayed! Admittedly it was an angry prayer revealing some of the poison which had invaded his relationship with God, but at least he prayed. That was certainly an advance on running away as he had previously done. But in other ways his prayer shows the marks of what we might call *spiritual infantile regression*. Just as in natural life the approach of a crisis, or the weight of a burden seems to force some people back into childish and inappropriate forms of behaviour for mature adults, the same can happen in the spiritual realm. Jesus' illustration of his own generation being like children playing in the marketplace springs to mind. They call out to other children:

> We played the flute for you, and you did not dance; we sang a dirge, and you did not mourn. For John came neither eating nor drinking, and they say, 'He has a demon.' The Son of Man came eating and drinking, and they say, 'Look at him! A glutton and a drunkard, a friend of tax collectors and sinners!' Yet wisdom is justified by her deeds (*Matt.* 11:17–19).

We have all witnessed similar events. Children go into a huff so easily; they are constantly in need of satisfying their immediate desires and needs. When they are crossed in any way they want to be comforted. They want their own way! So did Jonah. He sat outside Nineveh, unwilling to concede the perfect goodness of God's ways, totally reluctant to rejoice over a scene that must have produced great joy in the presence of the angels. We can also hear him saying, 'If you won't do it my way then I'm not taking part!' He was 'in a huff' with God. 'I told you this would happen', he sulked, 'and that's why I didn't want to come in the first place' (*Jon.* 4:2).

It is now possible to assess Jonah's position. *Geographically* he was outside Nineveh; *chronologically* he was in days of revival; but *spiritually* he was almost back to square one again. *He was certainly defending what he had done before and beginning to dig himself into the spiritual pit of his former disobedience.* But so miserable has he become about both his obedience and his disobedience that, rather than see the matter through, Jonah would prefer to die. So he prays for a kind of divine euthanasia:

> Therefore now, O LORD, please take my life from me, for it is better for me to die than to live (*Jon.* 4:3).

And he asked that he might die and said, 'It is better for me to die than to live' (*Jon.* 4:8).

It is apparently possible to be present to witness the blessing of
God falling in enormous power and to long to be elsewhere – or
better, to be nowhere. Indeed, it is possible to be in this condition
and be a real child of God. What an enigma! And yet, it is a true
reflection of the spiritual debilities that some of God's children
know. Jonah was not the first to want to give up (see *1 Kings* 19:4–
5), nor was he the last (see *Luke* 7:20). *But God was not willing to
give him up.* That was, in all likelihood, why his misery was so very
miserable. Jonah was caught between the vice of his own self-will
on the one hand, and the strong hand of God on the other. The
more he pushed, the more God pressed. He was bound to remain
miserable until either he or God let go. He knew that God had no
intention of giving up! Furthermore, God was just about to take the
initiative to restore him once again.

Jonah had made a little make-shift tent to shield himself from
the burning rays of the sun. He sat in its shade and waited to see
what would happen to the city. Was he still hoping against hope
that the judgment of God might fall on these Gentile dogs in
Nineveh? But, obviously, his little building efforts were inadequate
to give him the kind of comfort he really needed. God saw his situation, and had compassion on him. He provided a plant which grew
over Jonah's head. Jonah, we read, was 'exceedingly glad' (*Jon.* 4:6).

There is some debate about the nature of this plant, and the
translations offer a variety of alternatives: a gourd (AV) and a vine
(NIV) are among the suggestions. But the ESV footnote is surely
right when it suggests that this Hebrew word, *qiqayon* should be
translated 'the castor oil plant'. One needs to know no Hebrew to
recognize the appropriateness! It was just what Jonah needed – a
good dose of castor oil! Jonah certainly became attached to it: he
was thrilled about it (verse 6), and in a sense he loved it (verse 10).

No wonder, for it was the only companionship he allowed himself. Perhaps as he lay under its shade he began to speak to it, rehearsing his experience, chiding God for his dealings with him. He might even have given it a name – *Qiqi* the castor oil plant! Did he think that, like the ship at Joppa, it was a sign that God was indifferent to his disobedience and rebellion?

Early next morning, God sent a worm to destroy the plant. When Jonah awoke he must have thought he had slept in, it was so warm. But as he rubbed the sleep out of his eyes and began to get his bearings, he sensed that something was not right. The plant! Where was his shade? It lay in the sand beside him, maimed, gnarled, and as dead as dead could be.

In the meantime God had sent a scorching east wind that swept the sun like a furnace on to Jonah's body. He became angry and wanted to die. Why was God playing these games with him, one minute giving him shelter, the next exposing him to the rigours of the sun? He was angry now about his call, about his experience in the Mediterranean, about the way God had used him in Nineveh – and to crown it all he was as angry as death about this plant. That was the last straw!

Were we Jonah's personal pastor, we would take him by the shoulders and say to him: 'Do you not see that God is trying to say something to you through all these events?' For there is a clearly discernible pattern throughout this book which sounds like an echo in its chapters. We saw in chapter 1 how the summons of the pagan sea-captain must have served as a reminder of the original call of God: 'Arise . . . call out' (compare *Jon.* 1:2 with 1:6). Then, the word of the Lord which came once returned to him (compare *Jon.* 1:1 with 3:1). Further we should notice the way in which the whole book registers the providences of God. Four times the verb 'appointed' is used of God: he appointed the fish (*Jon.* 1:17), the plant(*Jon.* 4:6), the worm (*Jon.* 4:7) and the wind (*Jon.* 4:8). These were all the providences of God by which he intended to draw Jonah back into fellowship with himself. They certainly fulfilled their function in bringing Jonah's controversy with God to a head. By the last paragraphs of the book, *Jonah was shouting at God*. It was precisely then that God smote his conscience one last time:

> You pity the plant, for which you did not labour, nor did you make it grow, which came into being in a night and perished in a night. And should not I pity Nineveh, that great city, in which there are more than 120,000 persons who do not know their right hand from their left, and also much cattle? (*Jon.* 4:10–11).

Despite all the picture lessons God had given him, had he not yet learned the lesson that the immortal souls of men are the most precious thing in the universe? Yet he, Jonah, was worked up to screaming point because of the loss of a plant and the discomfort of the sun. Shame on him! Shame!

Jonah was a discredit to the name of the God of grace he professed to serve. God had now sent his last messenger of providence. The word of the Lord had now come to Jonah *a third time*. Now Jonah must decide: Disobedience or Commitment?

We simply do not know which time God speaks to us will be the last time. We do well to assume *this time* is the last time – and commit ourselves to the Lord while he still speaks.

# MISSIONARY EXPERIENCES

*But it displeased Jonah exceedingly, and he was angry.* [2] *And he prayed to the* LORD *and said, 'O* LORD, *is not this what I said when I was yet in my country? That is why I made haste to flee to Tarshish; for I knew that you are a gracious God and merciful, slow to anger and abounding in steadfast love, and relenting from disaster.* [3] *Therefore now, O* LORD, *please take my life from me, for it is better for me to die than to live.'* [4] *And the* LORD *said, 'Do you do well to be angry?'* [5] *Jonah went out of the city and sat to the east of the city and made a booth for himself there. He sat under it in the shade, till he should see what would become of the city.* [6] *Now the* LORD *God appointed a plant and made it come up over Jonah, that it might be a shade over his head, to save him from his discomfort. So Jonah was exceedingly glad because of the plant.* [7] *But when dawn came up the next day, God appointed a worm that attacked the plant, so that it withered.* [8] *When the sun rose, God appointed a scorching east wind, and the sun beat down on the head of Jonah so that he was faint. And he asked that he might die and said, 'It is better for me to die than to live.'* [9] *But God said to Jonah, 'Do you do well to be angry for the plant?' And he said, 'Yes, I do well to be angry, angry enough to die.'* [10] *And the* LORD *said, 'You pity the plant, for which you did not labour, nor did you make it grow, which came into being in a night and perished in a night.* [11] *And should not I pity Nineveh, that great city, in which there are more than 120,000 persons who do not know their right hand from their left, and also much cattle?'* (Jon. 4:1–11).

'Therefore now, O LORD, please take my life from me, for it is better for me to die than to live' (*Jon.* 4:3). We must now ask the leading question: How could a man who had seen God's power the way Jonah had, come to such suicidal notions? The parallel of Elijah can be cited, but even it shows Jonah in a poor light. After all Elijah had been very jealous for the reputation of God, and he had been threatened with death (*1 Kings* 19:2); he was exhausted and needed rest. We can understand Scripture telling us 'Elijah was afraid' (*1 Kings* 19:3). But Jonah has not presented himself to us as an unblemished hero. Nor was Jonah merely depressed; he was angry and arguing with God. What explanation can there be for this?

In fact, God was bringing Jonah to a point at which what was in his heart would come out of his lips. He was wanting to teach him that it is not what goes into our lives that causes defilement, but what comes out of our hearts. It is very significant that it was to the Pharisees that Jesus had to teach this elementary spiritual lesson (*Mark* 7:15). In Jonah's case God was intent on driving out every vestige of that same pharisaical spirit.

The Pharisees were originally a kind of 'holiness movement' within the Jewish church. In theology (by contrast with the Sadducees) they were conservative, and in moral issues they were deeply concerned for consistency and purity. Scriptural, practical holiness was their original intention, and personal piety the means of securing it. But by the time of our Lord many Pharisees were in grave danger of concentrating on externals and practising an external holiness. Some of them were 'whitewashed tombs' (*Matt.* 23:27). They had no heart of grace towards their fellow men. Most of these elements can be seen in the life of Jonah. They can be seen too in an 'orthodoxy' which is concerned only about outward behaviour patterns and unconcerned about the deep work of God in the heart.

If there is a special danger for professing Christians today, it must certainly be indifference to and ignorance of the true nature of the human heart! How easily outward behaviour and established patterns of belief can hide from us the true need we have for a new heart which beats in time with the heart of God! We should never be deceived into thinking that outward conformity to group norms, professions of conversion, or intellectual assent to orthodox doctrines are the same thing as a true heart knowledge of God. No amount of love for patterns of truth is exactly the same thing as love for Christ. It is possible to have a doctrinally pure church which has excommunicated apostles of error, and yet to be spiritually moribund – at least, this is the inspired conviction of the ascended Christ (cf. *Rev.* 2:1–7). His words should serve as lasting warnings to Christians whose hearts are set on pure doctrine and upright moral behaviour. These things are entirely biblical and laudable in themselves. But that is not the only issue. There is another issue: Do these things spring from and lead to a present experience of fellowship with and knowledge of God? Jonah was only now discovering how much it was possible to experience and to accomplish, and yet for areas of his life to be untouched by God's grace.

Jonah's trauma might well be called *The Missionary Experience*. Taken out of his normal home context, working under pressures never before encountered, sensing the frustration of a new culture and language so different from his own – these can bring the very worst out of a person, and often do. Sensitivities appear that are hitherto unknown, or could be hidden in our Christian fellowship at home. The bold knight errant who rides into foreign parts with high aspirations and expectations of fervent evangelism, of a ministry teaching the indigenous church, may soon find out that God has removed him across the face of the earth more for the sake of his own sanctification than that of others! There he may find what a narrow-minded, prejudiced, conceited, prayerless, fruitless, and uncooperative believer he really is in his heart of hearts; as a missionary once shared with me, 'I never knew what a heart of stone and filth I had until I went overseas.' In these circumstances a man or woman may be found confessing with Robert Murray M'Cheyne: 'The seeds of all sins are in my heart, and perhaps all the more dangerously that I do not see them.'[1]

This is exactly what we see in Jonah's experience, and it underlines one of the cardinal lessons of Christian service: when the ministry God has called us to exercise is fulfilled and our service has produced abundant fruit, God has not finished his task. He still has his servant to deal with, for he is more concerned with his servants than he is about their service. As we examine Jonah's experience in this light, there are several elements in it – of different degrees of intensity and importance – which demand consideration:

## THE SITUATION

We have already emphasized that it was not the circumstances in which Jonah found himself that caused his rift with God. But they did provide the catalyst for his response. They were like dry wood when the fire of sin was aflame in his heart. They do not excuse Jonah, but they help us to come to a clearer judgment of his life. His condition was partly a *reaction* to his situation.

How we *react* is often a better thermometer of our heart than how we act. Jonah was certainly reacting – for example, to the mental, physical and spiritual exhaustion of the last few days. They had tested his resources (already well-spent) and perhaps contributed to the dogged irrationality of his behaviour towards God. After all, he had been on the run; he had been overtaken by a near fatal storm; hours of darkness in the belly of the fish had followed his nightmare in the sea. Then there was the journey to Nineveh – and

[1] Andrew Bonar, *Memoir and Remains of Robert Murray M'Cheyne*, 1844, 1892; reprinted London: Banner of Truth, 1966, p. 153.

that solemn message he had preached. It is no surprise then that we find him an emotionally jaded figure as he sits outside Nineveh.

Jeremiah went through a similar experience. He had determined to speak no more in the name of the Lord. God's word was like a fire within him, and he had suffered quite enough. He could take it no longer:

> Cursed be the day on which I was born! The day when my mother bore me, let it not be blessed! Cursed be the man who brought the news to my father, 'A son is born to you', making him very glad. Let that man be like the cities that the Lord overthrew without pity; let him hear a cry in the morning and an alarm at noon, because he did not kill me in the womb; so my mother would have been my grave, and her womb forever great. Why did I come out from the womb to see toil and sorrow, and spend my days in shame? (*Jer.* 20:14–18).

Sheer physical exhaustion may wear out a man's sensitivity to God. That is why the plant God provided had a dual function. God was, as we have seen, speaking powerfully to Jonah through it. But he was also caring for him. Jonah needed the shade; he needed the rest. But God knew that he needed something more. Rest without repentance is never adequate.

## MYSTERY

Before considering some of the other contributory factors to Jonah's complex rebellion, we ought to recognize the presence of an element of *mystery* in it. One wonders if any servant of God really understands what he is saying when he speaks as Jonah did. But understanding *why* we react to God in this way is often beyond human diagnosis (which is why biblical preaching, in which the Holy Spirit applies God's Word to our hidden needs, is a more basic form of counselling than what we often call 'pastoral counselling'). When God moves in great power there are occasions when men are used in extraordinary ways, and may even seem to reach extraordinary degrees of godliness of life. But in the aftermath they appear very ordinary, very human. It is too superficial a reading to explain their condition exclusively by 'sin'. There is an element of mystery which teaches us not to profess to be wiser than we really are.

## CONFLICT

In the light of the full New Testament revelation we are able to see that the hand of a sinister foe touches the story of Jonah's life here.

Martin Luther used to speak about an experience that sometimes followed his service of Christ: 'The devil rode upon my back.' It is a vivid picture of a painful experience in the Christian pilgrimage. Luther knew what it was to be mightily used, and then to begin to feel the desires and affections he had put at God's disposal being turned in a direction which was hostile to the Lord – as though the reins of his spirit were being handled by a malignant force. The dying embers of sin were being fanned into a flame when he least expected it. In a sense that is part of the price we pay for being involved in Christian work.

We easily forget that we are not wrestling with flesh and blood, but against spiritual powers (*Eph.* 6:12). As soon as we begin to make inroads into that kingdom of darkness there are bound to be repercussions of lasting significance as Satan counter-attacks. In Jonah's case, almost without realizing it, he had destroyed by his preaching the battlements of Satan's kingdom so long-established in Nineveh. The enemy of God and men must have been provoked to considerable jealousy. He could not regain Nineveh until generations later. But there was something he could do to spite the God who had brought forgiveness to the Ninevites. He could make a spiritual wreck of God's instrument! Moreover, he knew that there was room for manœuvring in the rubble of indwelling sin which lay dormant in Jonah's heart. So he set to work. The distaste for God and his kingdom which Jonah began to feel was, in part, the evidence of his usefulness.

The Christian who loses his taste for what God is doing must look to see *who,* as well as *what,* is dulling his palate.

## PREJUDICES

It is impossible to discount Jonah's ethnicity from his reaction. He was a nationalist of the most dangerous kind – one who believes not only in defending his own territory and living for the benefit of his immediate kinsmen, but who, as a consequence, has a spirit of antagonism towards others, and hopes that God shares his attitude. There is more to Jonah's reaction than homesickness. He had been prepared to go to Tarshish without too much thought! But it was Nineveh he hated. It was Nineveh he felt should be barred from the grace of God. How he hated these Gentile dogs!

The spirit of the nationalist in Jonah's case drove him into antagonism against God and against his fellow men. It is legitimate in the sight of God to love our kinsmen, as Paul did, and to give expression to the most deeply felt concern for their welfare (see *Rom.* 9:1–3). But hatred of others as a result is a crime against both God and man.

We are living in a period of a world-wide upsurge of nationalism. It is plainly discernible in the United Kingdom, but it is evident in every corner of the earth. Men feel they have lost their corporate identity and long to find roots. It may be that in the years to come this warning note from Jonah's experience will be an urgent one for us to hear. Churches must never be conditioned by national environment rather than by the word of the gospel. But the kind of prejudices, which come to the surface in waves of nationalism, lie in the heart at all times. Prejudices (that is, for the Christian, judgments and opinions which are formed without knowledge of the circumstances, and not from the standpoint of God's Word) can daily drive us from the love of our fellows and from the service of God. Our prejudices need to be exposed, just as they were in Jonah's life. Once exposed, they must be destroyed by grace.

## SIN

None of these considerations exculpates the prophet. In the final analysis his response to God was *sinful*. The mystery involved in it was *the mystery of iniquity* (see *2 Thess.* 2:7, AV). That was why God's stern cross-examination was so necessary to bring Jonah to his senses: 'Do you do well to be angry?' (*Jon.* 4:4, see also 4:9).

In a sense Jonah had committed exactly the sin that the Pharisees were later to commit. They distorted the grace of God into legalism; they made his unconditional love depend on restrictive conditions; they *disgraced* God! That is why Jesus' conflict with them was essential, for they were destroying the character of his heavenly Father and detracting from his reputation as love itself (see *Matt.* 23:1–36). Jonah was guilty of the same crime.

What Jonah wanted was a God made in his own narrow-hearted image; a God with his own prejudices who would only come into fellowship with sinners under certain restrictive conditions. There was an element of the devil's character in Jonah!

The prophet also knew that serving the true and living God, and allowing himself to be transformed into his image (see *Rom.* 8:29) was a costly way for him to walk. It would mean conforming to the image of a God who was even then willing to make himself of no reputation in order to let Nineveh hear of his grace. It would mean that Jonah too would need to be willing to make himself of no reputation (see *Phil.* 2:7, AV). Jonah sat outside Nineveh (why was he not in the afflicted city, ministering God's word, engaged in personal work and being a true servant of God?). He now faced the greatest decision of his life: *Was he willing to die to his own reputation?*

The question was all the more pressing because he would soon return to his own people. How could he face them with the news that through his preaching God had visited the camp of their enemies? His reputation would be in shreds.

There was another dimension to the situation too. His message to Nineveh had been: 'Yet forty days, and Nineveh shall be overthrown!' (*Jon.* 3:4). But Nineveh still stood, and looked as though it would stand for many years to come! Where did that leave Jonah in the sight of the Ninevites? We have understood their repentance to be real (as Jesus did, *Luke* 11:32), but perhaps Jonah wondered how long it would last. He was in no condition to have much confidence in the abiding benefits of his own preaching. He was, in a sense, caught between the arms of a vice which were closing in on him with frightening speed.

What of his reputation in Nineveh? What of his reputation in Israel? Nowhere in the book do we find any record that God had plainly said 'Yet forty days and Nineveh will be overthrown!' More than likely God's Word had been couched more in terms of a warning than a promise (see *Jer.* 18:7–10). Had Jonah overstepped himself? Was that aggravating the wounds he already felt?

Doubtless a mixture of memories and motives crowded upon him. Above all he must have returned to this thought: The reputation of the God of grace in Nineveh necessitated the loss of the reputation of Jonah in Israel. It is a pattern that reappeared in the life of that other voyager on the Mediterranean, the apostle Paul: for the reputation of the God of grace among the Gentiles necessitated the loss of the reputation of Paul in Israel. The blueprint is to be found in a greater than either Paul or Jonah, in

Christ Jesus: Who, being in the form of God, thought it not robbery to be equal with God: But made himself of no reputation, and took upon him the form of a servant, and was made in the likeness of men: And being found in fashion as a man, he humbled himself, and became obedient unto death, even the death of the cross (*Phil.* 2:5–8, AV).

The real question was this: Would Jonah be willing to be like Christ? Would Jonah be willing to die to self? The issue which faced him is well-expressed in these anonymous words:

The last enemy to be destroyed in the believer is self. It dies hard. It will make any concessions if only it is allowed to live. Self will permit the believer to do anything, give anything, sacrifice anything, suffer anything, go anywhere, take any liberties, bear any crosses, afflict soul and body to any degree – anything, if it can only live. It will consent to live in a hovel, in a garret, in the slums, in far away heathendom, if only its life can be spared.

This was the heart of the matter. It is always the heart of the matter.

> Lord Crucified, O mark Thy holy Cross
> On motive, preference, all fond desires
> On that which self in any form inspires
> Set Thou that sign of loss.
> And when the touch of death is here and there
> Laid on a thing most precious in our eyes,
> Let us not wonder, let us recognise
> The answer to this prayer.
>
> AMY CARMICHAEL

I I

# GOD *IS* LOVE

*But it displeased Jonah exceedingly, and he was angry. ² And
he prayed to the LORD and said, 'O LORD, is not this what I
said when I was yet in my country? That is why I made haste
to flee to Tarshish; for I knew that you are a gracious God
and merciful, slow to anger and abounding in steadfast love,
and relenting from disaster. ³ Therefore now, O LORD, please
take my life from me, for it is better for me to die than to live.'
⁴ And the LORD said, 'Do you do well to be angry?' ⁵ Jonah
went out of the city and sat to the east of the city and made
a booth for himself there. He sat under it in the shade, till he
should see what would become of the city. ⁶ Now the LORD
God appointed a plant and made it come up over Jonah, that
it might be a shade over his head, to save him from his discomfort. So Jonah was exceedingly glad because of the plant.
⁷ But when dawn came up the next day, God appointed a worm
that attacked the plant, so that it withered. ⁸ When the sun rose,
God appointed a scorching east wind, and the sun beat down on the
head of Jonah so that he was faint. And he asked that he might die
and said, 'It is better for me to die than to live.' ⁹ But God said to
Jonah, 'Do you do well to be angry for the plant?' And he said, 'Yes,
I do well to be angry, angry enough to die.' ¹⁰ And the LORD said,
'You pity the plant, for which you did not labour, nor did you make
it grow, which came into being in a night and perished in a night.*

*<sup>11</sup> And should not I pity Nineveh, that great city, in which there are more than 120,000 persons who do not know their right hand from their left, and also much cattle?' (Jon. 4:1–11).*

T he immediate purpose of the plant that God provided was to shelter Jonah from his discomfort:

Now the LORD God appointed a plant and made it come up over Jonah, that it might be a shade over his head, *to save him from his discomfort.*

In an earlier chapter we noticed that there are certain themes that reappear like echoes in the very wording of this book. We now come to the last of them. The word in Jonah 4:6 translated 'discomfort' (ESV) or 'grief' (AV) or 'misery' (NKJV) is the same Hebrew word which was used of the wickedness of the Ninevites in Jonah 1:2, and of the destruction which God had threatened in Jonah 3:10. Just as God protected Jonah through the plant, he had shown the same protection to Nineveh through his compassion and grace. The use of the expression is charged with significance. It is the last echo of the grace of God Jonah will hear.

As the narrative relates, the issue was brought to a head by the destruction of the plant. Jonah was 'exceedingly glad because of the plant' (*Jon.* 4:6), and felt 'pity' when it died (*Jon.* 4:10). So attached to it had he become that he seems to have been angry about its demise not only because it gave him shade, but because he had an indefinable interest in it, and was deeply grieved and disappointed by its destruction. The atmosphere was charged with emotional electricity as God spoke once more:

'Do you do well to be angry for the plant?' And he said, 'Yes, I do well to be angry, angry enough to die' (*Jon.* 4:9).

Then God spoke with unparalleled seriousness:

'Jonah! You did not make this plant grow. You exerted no labour in tending it. It is a creature of a day. If you feel so much concern for this plant, what about the immortal souls of the 120,000 people in Nineveh who have been created in my image, whom I have sustained in life to this day, whose destinies forevermore will be fixed by their response to your witness to me? If you care about this plant, should not I care about this city?'

By implication the significance for Jonah was this: Should you, Jonah, not care too? If you are angry enough to die because of this plant, should you not be compassionate enough to live for these people? The truth was that Jonah seemed to care more about plants than about people.

This was a devastating critique of Jonah's spiritual condition. But it raises an issue no less disturbing about our own lives as Christians. Could the same be said about us? Do we care more about the items in our gardens, the produce of our fields, or perhaps the contents of our garage, or home, than we do about our fellow men and women and the spread of the gospel to them? Do we care more, in the last analysis, about our own comforts and plans than about the evangelism of the world in our time? The statistics of our giving, or praying, or going in the cause of Christ throughout the earth provide embarrassing reading to the church. They raise very real questions about whether we have begun to rid ourselves of the 'Jonah syndrome'.

Our Lord has commanded us to 'Go into all the world and proclaim the gospel to the whole creation' (*Mark* 16:15). Do we respond to his command as Jonah did? Are we angry inwardly that God should impose upon us such a burden? If God is concerned, can we remain unconcerned?

The closing chapter of the story of Jonah is indeed enigmatic. It may well leave us asking the question: Whatever did become of him? We do not really know. The story is left unfinished. But, in fact, that is the whole point of its writing. We have examined it as a piece of biography set at a given place and time in history. But it is more than that. It is *also* a parable. It is shaped in the same way that our Lord's parables are – not only as a fascinating piece of history, but to force us to contemplate our personal destiny. It carries no conclusion because it summons us to write the final paragraph. It remains unfinished, in order that we may provide our own conclusion to its message. For *you* are Jonah; *I* am Jonah. We recognize ourselves in the story of this man's life. We stand together in need of the mercy of God to enable us, from this day on, to be obedient to his commands, and to live to the praise of his glorious grace. With Jonah we must learn to say:

> Praise, my soul, the King of Heaven,
> To His feet thy tribute bring;
> Ransomed, healed, restored, forgiven,
> Who like thee his praise should sing?
>
> Praise Him for His grace and favour
> To our fathers in distress;
> Praise Him still the same for ever,
> Slow to chide and swift to bless.
>
> Father-like, He tends and spares us,
> Well our feeble frame He knows;
> In His hands He gently bears us,
> Rescues us from all our foes:
>
> *Praise Him! Praise Him!*
> *Praise Him! Praise Him!*
> *Widely as His mercy flows.*

HENRY FRANCIS LYTE